FROM
DEMOTION
TO
PROMOTION

How to Move from **Trauma** to **Triumph**

Dr. Ralph L. Simpson

FROM DEMOTION TO PROMOTION

Published in the United States by Legacy Asset Book Program,
a division of an imprint of The Money Cheerleader LLC, Atlanta, Georgia.
Book design by The Money Cheerleader LLC. Cover Illustration
Copyright © 2023 by Gianna N. Brown

Library of Congress Control Number Cataloging-in-Publication. Data available
upon request.

ISBN: 978-1-7351162-6-6 eBook ISBN: 978-1-7351162-7-3

Printed in The United States of America.

Dedication

To my dad, the late Mr. Henry Simpson Jr., thank you for instilling in me the essence of hard work, resilience, and income generation. Having a front-row seat to your tribulations prepared me to be the most authentic leader I could be, whether experiencing the best or worst of days. Words alone cannot express my indebtedness to you. I miss and love you. Until I see you again, Godspeed.

To my mom, Ms. Roxie Simpson, thank you for your unending prayers, unconditional love, and unwavering support that only a remarkable woman could give. You have been an ever-present haven in my life. Although the media outrage was embarrassing, I hope your son's proceeding triumphs and legacy-changing ascension more than made up for any mishaps. Mom, I love you.

To my two children, Chandler and Skyla, you two rock my world each and every day. There is no order too tall or no battle too large when it comes to you two. My resilience stems from your existence. Everything I do is ultimately for you. You two are my legacy, my pride and joy. Becoming your father unveiled a magnified leadership and love. I encourage you to go farther and do better than I ever could. All of this is for you!

To my big bro, Mr. Henry J. Simpson, you're the best brother on earth. There is no one quite like you. Because of you, I can walk with my head held high, grateful to have a steady friend at my side through thick and thin.

To the Fellas, Al Ringer, Tony Owens, and Kevin Ware, thanks for always believing in me. Our cultivated brotherhood has been nothing short of amazing.

To Michael Thurmond, thank you for restoring me!! You extended the timely opportunity I needed, and rightfully deserved.

Acknowledgment

Without any hesitation, the personal and professional relationship I fostered with Gianna Brown proved an invaluable foundation for building this book-writing process upon. Undeniably, my transformational story could not have been intimately captured by any stranger or publishing house alone. No, that would prove a pale comparison. What I aimed to achieve was so much more.

As I reviewed each chapter, it seemed like Gianna and her team personally walked a mile or two in my shoes, right there with me every step of the way. Not only was recounting my journey's traumas and victories extremely therapeutic throughout this whole process, but it also proved to be one of my life's most enriching experiences. I trusted the process, and your company delivered beyond my expectations. Thanks for being an astute student, remarkable visionary, and consummate leader.

FROM DEMOTION TO PROMOTION

DR. RALPH L. SIMPSON

Foreword

By Norman Thomas Jr.
Senior Pastor, First Baptist Church of Gresham Road

The greater the test, the greater the testimony.

Those words echoed in my mind as I read *From Demotion to Promotion.* As this book conjured up emotional and professional plights faced by millions, it vividly spoke to the transformative power inherent in our struggles. Echoing the age-old wisdom that there is nothing new under the sun, it offers a deep dive into navigating personal odysseys. Riddled with trials and sprinkled with triumphs, such learning encounters closely mimic similar waters charted by historical figures. Those who rose to iconic levels never did so without pushback or attacks. Reminiscent of biblical leader Joseph, an enslaved person who rose to be an extraordinary Egyptian leader, the retelling of a life-altering trauma unfolds. This written memoir underlines the universal themes of patience and faith. At the intersection of one's greatest ascension, turmoil emerges, and only those committed to their life's purpose survive.

Dr. Ralph Simpson, a figure of unwavering faith, embodies leading virtues through the narrative of his own life. Marked by tremendous adversity and rare victories, his testimony is a beacon for anybody seeking to live a meaningful life. It is a profound exploration of transcending the nature of traumatic adversity. The writing style eloquently demonstrates how setbacks can catalyze significant personal and professional growth. Provided insights inspire perseverance while offering a roadmap to navigating life's lowest points. Whether climbing the ladder of success or grappling with defeat, his career rollercoaster is a guiding light, encouraging us never to throw in the towel.

Dr. Simpson's story underscores the importance of taking action, demonstrating how even small daily efforts can lead to monumental results. From the first chapter, the reader is given an open invitation to discover key parallels in their own journey as his unfolds. Such introspection underscores personified integrity, resilience, and leadership against daunting odds. This powerful testament reminds us that, while we may confront certain challenges alone, the resulting strength and support propels us to new heights. Shared experiences highlight recurring themes of faith-filled resilience in the face of life's inevitable adversity. Each theme encourages us to see setbacks as opportunities for personal growth rather than barriers to better opportunities. Any inclination to believe glass ceilings are penetrable is evident throughout his life account.

Throughout each chapter, readers learn how conflicting moments are not just obstacles to be overcome. These hurdles are fresh opportunities to refine our character, enhance our leadership, and strengthen our resolve. His career blows extend beyond a mere comeback; it is about an extraordinary rise powered by unwavering standards and an indomitable spirit. As he emphasizes through internal dialogue and personal anecdotes, our darkest moments will inevitably sow the seeds of true leadership. Once planted, these deposits lead to our most illuminating accomplishments and reveal our true character.

Although this book is not merely a study of former conflicts or resolutions, it does provide applicable steps for readers to thrive amidst relentless tests. Such a literary platform empowers disruptive thinkers to resist any urge to quit. At pivotal moments, Dr. Simpson stood the course and emerged as a national, disruptive leader. Historical, revered opportunities were acquired in pursuit of his personal and professional fulfillment. Unfortunately, achievements are rarely free of painful growth opportunities. His life embodies the essence of turning trauma into motivation, showcasing that greatness remains tangible even in the most daunting circumstances. Each page of this book is a testament to the human spirit's capacity to overcome and ascend, setting a powerful example for all who seek to transform their trials into triumphs.

As I immersed myself in the pages of this book, the ancient Japanese art of Kintsugi kept running through my mind. This art form meticulously mends broken pottery with gold, thus celebrating the value of restoration. Each golden seam in Kintsugi is not just a repair; it's a symbol of survival and renewal, a resonating concept throughout the book. The Kintsugi philosophy and Dr. Simpson's teachings highlight the therapeutic benefits of embracing our fractured faith and painful scars. These elements are not mere reminders of past trials but are integral parts of our transformational story. His ability to transform life's adversities into sources of strength reminded me that broken spirits cannot place a permanent stronghold on those called by God.

Dr. Simpson's clarity and conviction shine through in every role he assumes, from a book writer to a guest speaker or corporate leader. His approach as a speaker is a blend of insightful storytelling and practical, actionable advice. When he speaks, a palpable energy resonates with everyone in the audience. Whether addressing a small seminar or large conference, he possesses the unique ability to connect with listeners, weaving his personal experiences with universal truths that speak to the challenges and aspirations of his audience. His speeches are brilliantly crafted, balancing the analytical with the emotional. Each attendee leaves with a clear takeaway that can be applied in their professional and personal lives. This same approach translates to his writing style as well.

By delivering words from a sincere place, Dr. Simpson's messaging provides more than just inspiration. Interweaving practical advice and personal insights, any approached thesis is transformative. As a national leadership icon, those working under his mentorship or reading his latest publications will further fortify their sense of self. This book is an award-winning memoir blended with a comprehensive toolkit. For anyone aiming to climb to new heights, read this one twice. It will help you clarify your path, prepare for adversity, and polish your standards.

This foreword is penned with the hope that it will illuminate paths for those learning how to maximize each day with grace and determination. As you embark on your own journey of overcoming and growth, be empowered to transform your breaking points into success milestones. Allow Dr. Simpson's story to serve as a constant reminder that by mending our traumatic breaks with the gold of wisdom and resilience, we repair and enrich our lives, turning every test into a powerful testimony. The path to greatness is often paved with trials, but our resilience, faith, and standards define our route. May you discover true inspiration to overcome obstacles as you gain behind-the-curtain access to Dr. Simpson's story. Embrace your life's calling with renewed vigor and purpose. Be blessed in your endeavors.

To Dr. Ralph Simpson, you are a resounding exemplar of humble leadership. You may have lost a battle or two, but please know you won every war that mattered. I commend you for being an undefeatable soldier in the army of the Lord.

Table of Contents

Introduction

Much like any noteworthy legacy gracing history books or modern influencers dominating the social media world, prominent leaders are not built overnight. The sacrificial rent to attain and sustain this headship is due on time every day over multiple decades. Reflect on the lifestyle price tag paid by any independent adult. Although paying monthly expenses on a personal residence or vehicle may seem exorbitant, it is an undeniable necessity for most people. Hence, paying the daily rent associated with headship carries an even heftier note comprised of time, energy, and intellectual power investments. If you are excessively late forking over the funds for any house or car, then you may be forced to forfeit the aspiring title or deed to your prized possessions unless you can cover the accrued penalties. Likewise, to lack sufficient, protective maintenance for your hard-earned leadership could result in similar outcomes. However, unlike physical possessions, any position attained is not easily reinstated if taken away. Trust me. I learned a thing or two about that after penning my first book. Within the pages of this new book you now hold, you will discover my story and learn how to rebuild after the destruction: beauty from ashes, if you will.

Peruse any digital library or grab a hard-cover encyclopedia. Discover that people of great stature never reigned for eternity. These constructs, like ancient empires started eons ago and modern multibillion-dollar corporations, were founded by larger-than-life individuals who were adept at leading. These visionaries undoubtedly experienced their fair share of rises and falls. This dichotomous journey is laced with strenuous objectives, lofty expectations, and admirable accomplishments. At the pinnacle of a leader's reign, when mind-boggling opposition transpires, it is difficult to envision a blossoming future.

For a first-world country like America, no one ever fathomed our great nation crumbling into a towering hill of ashes. Yet, our largest metropolitan area crushed those rose-colored glasses. Take a quick moment to reflect on the residual, traumatic impact of the Twin Towers attacks in New York on September 11, 2001. During catastrophic events such as these, millions turn to their leaders to provide hopeful direction. Such defining moments remind voters and followers of the dire necessity for well-rounded, strong leaders. Yet, once the divisive dust settles and daily life resumes, the arch nemesis's spirit of destruction resurfaces. No seasoned leader or acting president seeks these coveted positions expecting their feet to be swept out from under them. The pain of being dethroned cuts deeper than a fresh lashing across your back.

There is nothing new under the sun. Whether a queen, king, president, CEO, or captain of a sports team, each presiding official has had their positions threatened, robbed, or replaced. A leader is not only defined by their ability to lead during the good times but also during the less favorable ones. To take up the heavy mantle of any leading role requires a strong work ethic, a willingness to get your hands dirty, to serve as well as lead, and to make sacrifices when necessary. Assigned titles and acquired degrees do not fully embody the diverse spectrum of what being a true leader embodies. At the end of the day, these extra titles added to one's birth name are only activated potential when virtuous deeds ensue. Otherwise, they are merely words backed by trumped-up student loans. Sure, they add weighted color to a resume, but the real definition of a leader is much more complex.

While some individuals seek college degrees and accolades to gain a seat at the table and better opportunities, it is only a start. When the true test of someone's integrity and grit comes, the fire will either burn them (and their paper degrees) or cleanse them (like refining precious metal). During these defining seasons of struggle, one's ability to be stoned in the public eye while shielding one's immortal legacy from being stoned to death is a true leader signature. This person will use the jagged earth sediments to reconstruct a new, improved version of themselves planted on an unshakeable foundation, all the while without losing sight of their life's mission.

Extraordinary leadership is amplified during extreme times. At various stages of life, forerunning change agents must never remain dormant nor run from life-altering adversity. This self-development work is a leadership masterpiece that encourages trailblazers to boldly lean into adversity. In fact, chapter by chapter, readers will become equipped with proven tools. Are you the head person in charge or an informal leader regarded by the masses? If so, prepare yourself because challenges, sometimes backbreaking ones, will undoubtedly arise. This highly probable projection is not to instill any degree of worry or fear but to ensure that you understand the commonly touted phrase, "*to whom much is given, much is expected.*" This plays out ten-fold for heads of organizations, be it a well-oiled household or a corporate construct.

Most leaders adhere to written and unstated expectations, hoping and praying that the thin line they walk just by being human does not break as they cross over a jungle of hungry alligators waiting to take a huge bite at their shining excellence. These metaphorical alligators present themselves in many guises. Maybe they are jealous competitors lingering to take you down or once-trusted allies who have turned their backs on you. These predators can also be unfortunate circumstances that are no one's fault, simply being in the wrong position at the wrong time.

Switching gears, another overarching purpose of this second book, is to give a candid purview of the trauma associated with falling from a leading place of greatness. How do I intend to do this? Well, to be frank, I aim to clearly rectify the fraudulent characterization of my identity. Yes, you read that right. Fraud. We live in a world where identity fraud is common, but what I desire to vividly unpack is the gut-wrenching attack on my very character. The debilitating side effects go well beyond the mere stealing of my name, social security number, or excellent credit score advantages. My blemish-free integrity was questioned and put up to the firing squad.

As each page of this script is peeled back, my reading audience will delve into a firsthand account of the tragic events that led to my publicized demotion, followed by the subsequent action steps I employed to regain and supersede my personal evolution. It is now my turn to set the record straight once and for all. This manuscript aims to provide clear insights into an illegitimate book scandal, showing you who I really am, how I lead, and why I continued to fight the good fight. Despite challenging circumstances that threatened to undo all the transformational hard work I invested, I leveraged my unwavering work ethic to conquer each chastening hurdle. Justice would be served, one way or another. I made sure to have my rightful day in the people's court.

Prior to an isolated, bleak plot twist in my career trajectory and comfortable lifestyle, I was diligently upgrading the narrative of what it means to be a Black man in the United States of America in the 21st century. Parallel to any solid tale, my story was filled with conflicting turns and laudable promotions due to my resilience to overcome. Once I arrived at the climax, the goal was out of what should have been an impactful position, followed by a peaceful retirement. But this was not to be. An unpleasant surprise threw a wrench into this plan, and a new story unfolded.

Not only was I managing a workforce of 200-plus educators, earning six figures, taking care of my family, acquiring degrees, and empowering my community, but I was also authoring books like Georgia's own Dr. Narvie J. Harris, a prolific educator. Within the first year of self-publishing my first written work, I surpassed the 1,000-books-sold mark, a milestone only achieved by a handful of authors. The average self-published author is projected to reach 250 book sales if they are lucky. My burgeoning writing career was coming to an impactful fruition, the concrete achievement etched on my long bucket list. From leaders to families to non-profits across this great nation, readers gleaned the power of beating the odds. Students prone to acquire higher rates of literacy and graduation diplomas were on the rise. The future was primed with potential for further reach, and I stood at the peak of my mountain of success.

From Demotion to Promotion

Ralph Simpson was no longer merely the name my parents, Roxie and Henry Simpson, had chosen for my birth certificate one December day or the name engraved on my office desk plate underscored with the title, high school principal. No, it was a nationally recognized symbol of education reform. Outside of the befitting name denotation of courageous counselor, my name, Ralph or Simp, was a highly respected, well-known brand. Beyond my entrepreneurial ventures linked by the common mission of community empowerment, I had high aspirations of becoming the district's next superintendent given my lengthy tenure. That position would extend my reach and further enhance long-overdue educational initiatives. It seemed the next obvious advancement, after all. From the mountaintop view I had, nothing seemed impossible with the right mindset and work ethic. Awestruck by the rocky territory I had scaled to reach this rare elevation, I could honorably recount my career hike. Each promotion obtained did not result from nepotism but from operating as an honest, hardworking administrator with a heart for the people. No glass ceiling, whether in human or paper form, could block me from climbing to the next pinnacle.

But first, indulge me for a quick moment as I provide a clarifying backdrop to the most notorious fall of DeKalb County leadership. Perhaps then you will understand better why events unfolded as they, regrettably, did. For years, the education industry balked at the idea of putting Black men in a place of

7

authority. In fact, the School Superintendents Association conducted a survey and found that only 11% of superintendents identify as Black or African American. Mirroring the hierarchical designs of Corporate America, high-ranking jobs like these were typically reserved for the white male. Fortunately, DeKalb County had fought to change that inequitable narrative by naming Crawford Lewis, an esteemed Black educator, as the superintendent in 2004. Despite the perpetuation of jarring statistics confirming Black school superintendents remains sparse to this very day, I decided to be the exception. My extensive résumé checked all the boxes to more than qualify: ten years as an educator, notable references, historical graduation gains, a clean record, and keen communication skills, just to name a few. Now, if the district was running on a meritocracy, then I was the perfect candidate.

Bygone days of backward thinking and white supremacy finally seemed a thing of the past in DeKalb County's executive leadership. Living in the 21st century, one would be inclined to optimistically cling to this equitable hope, especially given the southern hospitality associated with the Deep South. Yet, as you will learn, hospitality on a grand, public scale only extends as far as preconceived notions and outdated mindsets. Given a certain set of circumstances, politeness and false smiles are revealed for what they truly are: nimble minds easily shaped by the loudest, most popular voices.

For over twenty blessed years, I fomented a stellar and exemplary career as an educational leader. I never once had an unsatisfactory evaluation as a teacher, assistant principal, principal, or Regional Superintendent. So, what was the problem with aiming higher? Initially, there did not seem to be one looming on the ever-expanding horizon. The colors of educational empowerment and community engagement painted across that metaphorical sky were brilliant. I highly anticipated opportunities to add my brushstrokes to that canvas. My aspirations did not seem ridiculous or unrealistic, given my qualifications and experience. Now, this is not an effort to be pretentious but to merely highlight the dismissed facts. Remembering the goals one accomplished and confidently standing on those truths is paramount to climbing any corporate ladder. Onlookers and decision-makers look favorably upon a person who stands in that conviction. Given my career accomplishments and personal development, there was nowhere to go but up. Falling did not seem like an option as I planted my feet firmly on that peak and looked out over that horizon. I was literally living my best life, or so I rightfully projected.

"Work hard in silence;
let your success
make the noise."

Author Unknown

1

The Timely Ascension

In 2007, the No Child Left Behind Act, implemented by former U.S. president, George W. Bush, was still gaining momentum since its implementation in 2001. Finally, a nation founded on discriminatory practices started to understand that equitable educational experiences were paramount, especially to narrow daunting literacy gaps that had existed for decades. A scholar's ability to read and write above grade level would no longer be reserved for the top third of school-age students. Being literate was a competence that extended far beyond the classroom, dictating school climates and societal woes alike. Those possessing this survival skill not only exhibit the ability to read and write well. This skill set unlocks formerly closed doors, giving hope for future generations to exceed the limitations inherently placed on their parents and grandparents. Any devout guardian wants their children to go farther in life than them. Educators also desire this for the scholars who walk into their classrooms nine months every calendar year.

To combat this dismal fate, underperforming schools, typically housing marginalized groups, including Blacks and Hispanics, received additional incentives and resources to close the literacy gap by 2014. Title I grants allocated to high-poverty schools intercepted a financial infusion of $14.3 billion. Such a historically massive increase of 63% encouraged key decision-makers and stakeholders to take a closer look at learning through the lens of relevant reading experiences. I played an intricate role in this important historic undertaking. My benevolent heart palpitated with a deep-seated need to help these underprivileged kids who had done nothing wrong and who deserved just as much a chance at a successful, fulfilling life as anybody. Knowing this, my mind reeled with possibilities to create this reality and play my part as a cog in a larger wheel of achievement. To this promising light, a few select school leaders, including me, published their first books and fulfilled purchase orders for external schoolhouses, including burgeoning authors employed in DeKalb County. As leadership teams worked to appropriately allocate their annual budgets, with literacy in mind, purchasing bulk orders of literary works to serve as the official "book of the month" became a trending theme in numerous countries that extended far beyond metro-Atlanta school districts.

During this same transformative year, the sweltering summer served as an optimal time to add another title to my name: author, not simply for popularity but for societal necessity. Since beginning my tenure at Main Street Elementary, now E. L. Miller Elementary, in 1991, I noticed firsthand the engagement and academic performance gap between females and males in middle schools. Millions may have been engulfed in the Olympic games we were hosting in our city of Atlanta that year, but I was enraptured in positioning our students to experience life-changing wins within the schoolhouse. Would you believe that it was less than a hundred years ago that it became legal for Black people to pick up a book?

From 1740 to 1867, Southern states continued to limit disenfranchised people, both enslaved and free people of color. Literacy was weaponized as an anti-slavery antidote, thus cutting into plantation owners' bottom line. Any non-white person found reading or writing was sentenced to an unpayable monetary fine or a physically debilitating whipping. The pain extended far beyond the physical appearance. To be denied access to this basic ability was a stab to the mind's wellness and the heart's hope. It was another reminder of where they were told they belonged. However, the compassionate white allies who secretly tutored Black people were forced to pay a $500 fine, too, if caught. In 1865, that would have been over $9000! That was an exorbitant amount of money back then, as an acre of land only cost $1.25. Of course, some brave, wrongfully enslaved people risked it all to achieve this essential skill set for succeeding in the free world.

Fast forward, now that written, anti-literacy laws were eradicated, gifted authors like Howard University Alumna, Toni Morrison and Fisk University graduate, Dr. W.E.B. Dubois decided to reach the peak of literacy. From winning awards like the Anisfield-Wolf Book Award and John Leonard Prize, these renowned Black storytellers and civil rights activists bravely capitalized on accessibility to life's gold medal: literacy. Given groundbreaking accolades like these amid extreme racism, I etched a new law across my chest: help our students attain exceptional educational outcomes, literacy rates, and character traits. However, this was more than a law. It was a dream that would be realized. It was thinking outside the box that was still too often confined all these decades after Black people were given the freedom to read and expand their horizons. It was forging a newfound legacy that would outlive me for generations.

When we thoroughly assessed test data, males outperformed females in math or multiple-choice components, but females excelled more in reading and language arts. Could this be a leading indicator for the gender-graduation gap, illustrating that females graduate from public schools at a rate of 10% more than their male counterparts? As I delved into these numbers even further, I uncovered a brutally painful fact. While white middle schoolers showed a 44% literacy rate, Black boys, like me, only reached a 10% literacy rate. This was alarming. In turn, as reported by the Southern Regional Education Board, Black males achieved a staggeringly low 59% graduation rate. If I were without hope, I would have allowed that shock factor to zap my energy and give up. Yet, hope flowed through me like the hot blood in my veins. Why sit there and allow this depressing reality to prevail? Something had to be done, so I stepped up to the plate alongside other social reformists. This was a movement.

As I curiously dug deeper like a miner searching for gold hidden within the earth's underbelly, I committed to identifying the root cause of this national epidemic. This research became personal because I frequently realized that if it had not been for devout parents like Mr. and Mrs. Simpson, I might have fallen into this very conundrum that trapped many young Black men. Academics were not discussed daily, but these two expected me to handle business in the schoolhouse. Occasionally, they would tell my brother and me, "You better get your lesson." I understood that I had better meet the necessary requirements for promotion. During my formative youth, those two high school graduates consistently encouraged me to win the pizza awards by reading a predetermined quantity of books within a specific timeframe. Although I was far from an avid reader, I reveled in the opportunity to make those two flash their approving smiles and get a hot cheese pie as my reward. It was a double win for me as a young man. Then, as I continued my research, it dawned on me that reading competencies were truly fundamental, more specifically in the ninth grade. This nine-month span had the potential to set a positive or negative life trajectory for every student entering a high school's doors. In fact, The University of Chicago Consortium on School Research found that students who successfully complete the required ninth-grade courses are more likely to graduate from high school than those who fail one class or more. As backed by qualitative and quantitative data gathered across high schools, these results led this consortium to deem freshman year as the "make-it-or-break-it" year. That said, how could a student be expected to cross the graduation stage if the love lost for reading was never recaptured? Simply put, they could not. Another name would be added to daunting dropout statistics and on my watch as an educator. I could not allow this possibility to chokehold another generation.

To lessen the life-changing effects of being illiterate, I decided to pen a book for my younger self. I reviewed my personal budget and set aside four thousand dollars to self-publish this work. While I had ample funds in my splurge account to hire professional editors and illustrators, I found it more rewarding to sow financial seeds into my friends' pockets. Former coworkers and current friends pitched in to illustrate and proofread for a nominal fee. Like a *JET* magazine, a weekly publication highlighting culture, entertainment, and news pertinent to the

African American community, my book would narrow the literacy gap one reader at a time. Unlike an entertainment magazine, my book would play a vital role in shaping children's futures. As a grocery shopper prepared for checkout, he or she could peruse the real-life anecdotes embodied in this short read. From solving problems to overcoming external challenges, the protagonist channeled his inner gifts and resilience to matriculate to each grade. In time, this scholar beat the odds, attained a few college degrees, and set out to be an educational inspiration. It was my hopeful dream that this story would drive the readers to follow a similar success path, every footstep being one in the right direction. Reading material can prove both fun and didactic, and students learn best when the content-rich book is relatable, hence learning without even knowing it!

As Regional Superintendent, I ascended the corporate ladder from my starting leadership step as an assistant principal in 1996. A decade later, I was even more vested in positive student outcomes. Therefore, at the peak of my career, I stepped away for the summer holiday season granted to those in the education field. I put the finishing touches on my first book and held my breath as I released it to the world. Like a child leaving home and heading to college for the first time, I had high hopes for my written contribution to the world. Before long, journalists and public relations agents started featuring me in their newspapers, and even the big-time *Good Day Atlanta* booked me for a candid conversation. In time, my phone was ringing more frequently than 911 calls during off-school months. From being the keynote speaker at conferences to helping scholarship committees select the best beneficiary, I was a much sought-after professional. Such a popularity boom amplified my book's voice and business reach. My climb to greater heights was in the limelight, broadcast across national platforms. I was now taking off in flight from that mountaintop. This was the long-awaited kick-starter to reach new heights and larger audiences.

Takeaways — Lend A Hand As You Ascend

Progressive leaders are resourceful, intelligent, and see beyond the moment. Similarly, a person's ability to fully engage their leadership capacity as tides and titles change is critical for survival. They understand what they have built, are building, and will continue to build and rebuild. A leader's legacy will survive well beyond their earthly years. Rising to more noteworthy, higher levels in the earthly realm is a truly gratifying experience. Wherever you are in life at this current moment, one underlying truth is that your ascension can be credited to a former, ambitious multitude. It is a resounding domino effect. Each one of us stands on the shoulders of greats, whether we realize it or not. Close your eyes and breathe in a fresh breath of humility for a second. Remember those with newfound gratitude who came before you and who helped you arrive at this momentous point. You may have had that special teacher who spoke life into you. Maybe it was a coach who lent a space for you to display your gifts. Perhaps it was a leader who told you to walk in your higher calling. From breaking barriers to challenging the status quo, someone fought to ascend with the hopes of giving you a more favorable starting point in life's marathon. They looked on with proud smiles and tears of joy as they watched you cross every successful milestone. These great leaders led households, boardrooms, schools, businesses, and other organizations in rewriting tired old defeat narratives. Each day, such leaders decided to carve higher standards into this great nation's stone, skillfully weaving transformative threads into America's fabric. What pictures were they crafting? Do you see your pivotal role in the promising imagery?

Now, the torch has passed to you. It is your turn to be those shoulders to catapult the next generation to even better outcomes. The tides turn, and days march on. There is no time to sit on the sofa and immerse yourself in countless hours of Netflix binge-watching or virtual reality video games, stuffing your face with junk food and alcohol. Each waking minute is a fresh opportunity to ascend to your next level of greatness while reaching back to show a burgeoning leader how to do the same. Let us scale this leadership mountain together.

"The ultimate measure of a man is not where he stands in the moments of convenience and comfort, but where he stands at times of challenge and controversy."

Dr. Martin Luther King Jr.,
Prominent Minister and Civil Rights Activist

2

R.U.F.K.M. Tension

Despite the time and workforce required to build an organization or edifice, nothing under the sun is indestructible. Neither Rome, the Twin Towers, nor the world-renowned Egyptian pyramids were built during a single season by merely one individual. Over a two-decade period, the Great Pyramids of Giza required a committed, skilled labor force of 20,000 or more. While these ancient structures continuously eroded given earthly elements, New York's Twin Towers burned into smoldering ashes from cold-hearted terrorists. As a tense nation, we forewent our differences, collectively following our elected leaders. Day by day, we rebuilt after 9/11's destruction. With time, however, all things built by moral human beings will crumble. Nothing remains forever. Whether it be reconstructing a former edifice or reinforcing a solid structure withstanding time's long line, framing a new construct is a lengthy, often difficult process. Vision, time, and labor are all essential pillars.

In this same light, breaking the mold by building an education framework impacting today and future generations demands a revolutionary leader. To move outside of one's residing region and construct a resounding reputation impacting our globe's distinct corners is no doubt a lofty mission. From inception to completion, developing a holistic vision takes exorbitant amounts of time and resources, especially when your decisions may challenge the day's status quo. Being a leader is no small feat. Many are repulsed by such a grandiose job, but someone must do it. With this undertaking, requirements like integrity, hard work, dedication, a servant's heart, and an innovative mind are necessary.

When I entered the education industry, I did so under the guise of an alarming need for reform. Ranging from prevalent school-to-prison pipelines to inequitable school funding, a long list with several problems limits the efficacy of a technology-rich, evolving learning experience. Even as a novice leader, I made an immovable commitment that I would be a living resolve regarding these snowballing issues. In fact, I arduously invested twenty-plus years climbing the educational corporate ladder, dodging frivolous trends threatening to demolish key officials' historic track records. Unfortunately, even when solid structures of substances are built upon a solid foundation, a sizable, forceful attack can annihilate any construct, knocking it down in a solitary, quick-as-lightning blink. You can do everything right, exuding a premium work ethic and integrity. You can consistently empower and extend grace beyond borders, whether others seem deserving or not. Whether or not they are worthy, you cleave to authentic leadership's golden rule: Do unto others as you would have them do unto you. So, in that reciprocal vein, you would naturally expect others to treat you with the same respect. Such a logical conclusion should make sense, coming to fruition. Sadly, this is rarely how the real world turns. It continues to be an ever-changing terrain disproportionately rife with falsehoods, backstabbing, and unfairness. Then, when all is said and done, you observe such a gaping wasteland in the aftermath, then shake your head. Afterward, you sadly remember that a prestigious empire, one you worked so hard building, once graced an old spot. Then, your pivotal question becomes a matter of admitting defeat or persevering against the odds. What are you willing to give up or gain for your chosen path?

Now, imagine my complete, utter dismay when I witnessed the media publicly convey that I had committed a financial scandal. I was emphatically appalled as my stomach morphed into piercing army knots threaded with four-inch nails. How on earth would I circumvent such defeat? Life seemed unbearable. Any fluttering butterflies I had since beginning my leadership role were stirred deep within. These harmless imaginary insects metamorphized into furious hornets swarming after someone maliciously kicked their nest, dismantling their comfort zone like never before. Some disruptive force had certainly kicked my gut! Despite my natural inclination to worry or allow emotion to chokehold my perspective, I suppressed those natural urges. Immediately, I pulled away from my plush leather sofa and went toward my room. Within such a solace space's confines, I fervently entered prayer, questioning our heavenly Creator. Was He trying to show me a different (conceivably better) way? Was this a test of resilience or faith? Did He have a grander design for yours truly? These questions, plus fifty more, swirled relentlessly through my weary mind during those long, pensive hours shut in darkness. It was as if I was a modern-day David but from the ATL.

When David from Judah wrote various Psalms more than three thousand years ago, he, too, posed mounting inquiries with the hope of gaining a more profound understanding. Many Psalms are laments, our hearts' cries during wilderness seasons. Yet, within a crushed spirit of human brokenness, switching my perplexed perspective to a gratitude attitude was like an encouraging, illuminating North Star. A brave portion of my forcefully enslaved ancestors used this night light as a guiding compass to freedom above the Mason-Dixon Line. Now, I would use sincere gratitude as a guiding light through this dark tunnel of suffocating agony.

While it is certainly human nature to become bitterly angered or seek emotional damages by monetary compensation, intentionally counting blessings was my elected freedom tool going forward. I chose rising above. I chose joy over defeat. Yet, even cocooned in crisp, clean Egyptian cotton bed sheets, I could not sleep. Blissful slumber eluded me at every turn. Each time I dosed off, like a ten-ton whale placed on my chest, shortness of breath interrupted any chance I had of reaching deep-realm sleep. As a young child, elders advised me to count sheep or to one hundred until I fell asleep. Yet, as a grown man with adult responsibilities, I started listing people and opportunities I still had. Such a reflective method freed me from a few shackles figuratively placed around my throat. As my world burned down around me, I focused on what I still had before a public audience presented a chance to re-center myself. Despite my internal fury threatening to erupt like an emotional volcano, I concentrated solely and resolutely on God the Creator, and my children. It always pays well to glance at the world and stare at God.

Ladies and gentlemen, let me be crystal clear. I had no malicious intent or concealed desire to manipulate the very system I meticulously re-engineered to bring closer to meeting global standards of excellence. Moreover, two high-profile bishops who authored my book-in-question's foreword and final words would probably cast poor Simpson down to hell's deepest, darkest pits at the very instant I was guilty of an unethical action. Nonetheless, frequent reminders I was erroneously blindsided remained unceasing. It was nearly impossible to wrap my judicious mind around any rationale worthy of such unwarranted torment. Every other night, I beckoned God to reveal a valid purpose behind such emerging madness. Other times, I humbly asked for clear answers as to how such a disruptive nightmare had come to pass. Shortly after reaffirming these spiritual connections, I noticed my social circle dwindling as the coming weeks unfolded. An unfortunate truth presented itself: only real friends remain in your corner when the kitchen gets hot, underscoring these scanting relationships. Thankfully, I still had four favorite allies, trusty comrades ready to fight at my side, no matter what would come. Everyone needs such honest, true friendships. When all glitz and fame fall away, what remains is telling. Nothing else matters.

In lieu of agonizing isolation caused by swiftly distant relationships, my best friend and running partner, Randal Reid, stepped in, ensuring my physical well-being remained intact. You see, God works through other people. Randal was one of His timely vessels, my wise sounding board. As we hit three-to-seven-mile runs on Cascade Road across multiple weeks, Randal and I passed our invisible comeback baton. Engaging in profound vulnerability, I handed him inner thoughts, which ranged from defeated to empowered, just as unpredictable as Georgia's weather on any given day. It could be rainy on Monday, then sunny on Tuesday. Such is life. But I have now weathered a personal strong storm and unpredictable season change. Play by play, I recounted excessively damaging fallacies being conjured up against yours truly, making me into a targeted eyesore. It was as if seasoned soldiers were at a gun range doing target practice. No one missed their target either. Yes, I stood there, the brunt of their arrows, bullets, you name it. Each reputation-destroying bullet hit my heart at its core. Randal listened attentively as we reached the one-mile mark. I can still see the thoughtful expression on his face as we huffed, keeping pace. He never grew tired when I almost continuously poured my case's factual evidence.

August 2007 was now upon us. As the school session resumed, the buzz generated by my first book drew the attention of metro-Atlanta leaders, including the principal of one of my former high schools in a different region. That visionary principal was laser-focused on meeting every school improvement goal. For one, she considered academic gaps and inequities working against rising ninth graders. Since she knew my personal story of how I overcame scholastic challenges, she considered my book as a keen way to creatively spark these preteens' fleeting interest in academics. Likewise, students could possibly become better readers. Then, they could experience heightened literacy scores. After discussing her purchase order, I meticulously wrote down the next steps, ensuring a smooth transaction. First, I scheduled a meeting with my immediate supervisor, the then Deputy Superintendent. She glowed with elation when she learned that

Miller Grove High School wanted to purchase a bulk set of my books. Neither she nor I could find any issue with our transaction, especially since I no longer served as principal there. Additionally, this high school operated under a different regional superintendent. No conflict of interest there, I thought. No written conflict of interest policy existed. I assumed everything would be fine, more than fine. What reason did I have to believe otherwise? History had told a compelling, straightforward story thus far. Life had rolled along like a train on a smooth track.

Now, let us return to those defining runs with Randal. Once we reached our three-mile mark, I shared the second safeguard I employed to deter any raised eyebrows or future concerns. I double-checked with the office of compliance. Their executive issued a verbal approval, followed by a directive to email a copy of the transaction upon completion since I had brought it to his attention. After those two necessary approving stamps, final signatures were obtained. The Title I director, the Regional Superintendent, the principal, and I all signed off on the literary tool that would positively transform an incoming student body. My business shipped four hundred books to that seemingly lucky school's proud front doors. Such a win felt like a powerful vitamin B shot into my veins, surging through this young fellow with newfound momentum. This energy boost encouraged, energized, and invigorated me as I provided a solution for students who lacked a love for reading or literary arts. Like me, these students would rarely be found curled up deep within a cozy corner, engulfed in a book during their leisure time. Nine times out of ten, they would be found outside at basketball courts, joking around, shooting hoops, with dreams of being drafted to the illustrious NBA or playing at college level. Even with heavy breathing caused by sprinting, I could recount backward the fiduciary steps I took if needed. Remember, truth is always easier to recall than a lie.

Quickly after processing my shared information, we seamlessly eased into an Olympic-style pace. Randal exhaled deeply. He assured me everything would be okay, which he followed with a strong recommendation: "Simply trust the process. Be patient, brother".

As I allowed his positive affirmations to rest deep within my soul, I bravely received our proverbial hope baton back into possession. God truly does work in mysterious ways. Randal may not have realized his well-played pivotal role in my narrative, but he no doubt served as an answer to distressed prayers. To the naked eye, he never appeared belabored with my repetitive confessions accompanying our runs like additional joggers, determined as we were. For me, stating facts allowed reassurance that I did not commit a crime. Yes, I, without a doubt, had crossed all T's and dotted all I's, plus some. For that defining moment, I had a breath of fresh wind. Just successfully finishing our sprint proved quite therapeutic. This world's heavy, burdensome pressures detoxed through my profuse sweat, giving me a renewed gumption. Those jogs were just what I needed: a balm for deep wounds.

However, without fail, routine moments offering renewed hope were short-lived. Biased, ill-educated referees and commentators continued changing the rules of engagement, hitting my knees, and threatening to trip me up all over again. Eventually, each time I tied up my running shoes, a chastising hangman game commenced. This all-consuming book debacle wrapped a snug noose around my neck. How could I even breathe, let alone fight another day? Those proved defeatist thoughts. But I would not allow them dominance. Yet, such a thick, unforgiving rope steadily tightened as I fought to catch my breath and then face the next obstacle at hand. I felt like I slowly died as I hung in those glum gallows, a hanged man convicted of an imaginary crime, yet sentenced to an agonizing, albeit unjust, death. While I appeared to exhibit healthy exuberance outwardly, as if my soul remained perfectly tethered together, I was crushed.

Scrutiny mixed with internal agony proved harrowingly excruciating as it gnawed away, piece by tiny piece, at flesh. If I did not die from the invisible noose, I would surely perish from this monster devouring every vital organ, bleeding out all life, all hope. All that said, I am certain Randal's steady presence on those runs reignited an innate ability to keep my mental, spiritual, and emotional well-being intact. Even with all my cylinders firing, I egregiously fought to wrap my exhausted mind around such a painful trial as it escalated. Overnight, Lil Simp fought against this big, unforgiving, unfair, relentless, evil world. A total, brutal knockout lingered on the horizon. I proved ill-prepared. No easy recovery from this heart-wrenching fall could be fathomed. If only I knew how much further I would fall before hitting rock bottom or how many more character lynchings were brewing. Then again, at the base of even the deepest, darkest pit is the Rock, our Lord, the space to reaffirm your worth. How would I dig myself up from such a gaping hole? Not alone, that much would be for sure.

Takeaways — Paralyzing Shock Factor Hits

Cruising down any major highway in Atlanta, cars hit seventy miles per hour like daily clockwork. This is expected. It is nothing new, as sure as sunrise and sunset. The journey is a predictable route to and from a determined destination, typically transpiring without so much as a hitch. Occasionally, a driver will glimpse a lifeless deer injured beyond repair, lying at an emergency lane's edge. Many question why these lean white-tailed creatures fail to run from ensuing danger like they do upon hearing gunshots from hunters after this exact game. No, instead of darting for cover back into the deep forest, these brown-coated mammals freeze. The deer in headlights is an overused expression for a reason: because of its truth. Even with an average speed of thirty miles per hour, this mammal could escape imminent danger with little effort. Yet, they stand strong, placing their average 200-pound bodies toe to toe with a two-ton vehicle. Although their brain is only one-sixth the size of humans', perhaps these graceful animals believe their sheer size will defeat the oncoming predator. Leaping to safety is never employed. Unfortunately, at a bloody impact, the threatening force knocks life from them. If they survive, they are never the same, either from mental trauma or physical incapacitation. So, why does an animal at a huge disadvantage size-wise not run for cover? Why not use the resources, namely its speed, to save itself? Why do we, when we are at a major disadvantage, not employ our resources but often remain rooted in paralyzing fear? Good questions, friends. Because fear is strong, it smothers hope.

Well, for the first time, my love for running hung null and void. I understood danger and pain's paralyzing effects alike. Boy, did I ever. My legs fell limp as I stared at oncoming traffic aimed at mowing me down. When I heard about a brewing investigation from strangers' lips reading the news to thousands of households, I froze. Like the proverbial deer in headlights mentioned above, my heart skipped a beat. I involuntarily became immobile. My feet were cemented to a one-foot tile. I could not dash in any direction, no matter how hard I tried. I felt trapped in a nightmare. I was shocked; the headlines were blinding. A quick moment of amnesia made me forget my continued blessings: my experience, intellect, family, friends, colleagues, degrees, and good health. This spoke little volumes as I singlehandedly faced a behemoth of lies and accusations.

Whatever daunting challenges you may face, resist the urge to be consumed by negative emotions threatening your overall well-being. Choose the higher, progressive road. Before you give too much power to electrifying opinions and deliberations, reactivate your faith-filled dreams. Perseverance is vital. You must persist at all costs. Scaling your success ladder is a marathon, not a sprint. Give yourself permission to be the leader you need, not want. Rage and fear are energy-wasting distractors. Do not allow those self-defeating emotions to live rent-free within your remarkable mind. Stand before your mirror. Repeat this phrase: "Things are happening for me, not to me." While destructive crises upheave, find peace in knowing when blinding dust settles, you will still be standing. Tenaciously re-evaluate the bundle of gifts you can offer our world. Deep within your heart, you must find solace in knowing a defeating moment is not a fatal lynching of your future aspirations. Otherwise, others' opinions and verdicts will control your life. You cannot give power to such lies, especially when you have the world at hand. Drive your ship well, firmly, steadily toward hopeful horizons. Keep your feet firmly planted on solid ground. Dream big regardless.

"You don't lose if you get
knocked down;
you lose if you stay down."

Muhammad Ali,
Heavyweight Champion of Boxing and Activist

3

The Three-Tier Investigation

The United States Department of Justice was designed to create a more equitable and just society. This system is charged with managing a society to be a well-ordered topography. Dual-purpose entities like these render harsh consequences to criminals proven guilty in the court of law by an unbiased jury while granting freedom to those proven not guilty. From physically abusing innocent children to laundering substantial funds from retirement plans, this legal construct was intended to serve as a managerial tool for a populous nation inhabited by diverse people with staggeringly different motives. In this light, it should keep the good people protected from the devious acts of the small wayward minority. That withstanding, the judicial system has a legible, step-by-step process. When an actual law is broken, the suspect is entitled to a fair investigation and trial before sentencing.

Unfortunately, in a country still plagued with systemic racism and poverty well into the 21st century, this expected legal process is gravely reserved first for those who were born without brown skin. For these individuals, approximately 60% of the American population, a biased eye or an officer's prejudices automatically kick in. Instantly, before a trial and jury ever occur, a person of color is all too often sentenced to death or deemed guilty without any merit, intellect, or consciousness. The naked eyes transform into the judge and jury within a quick millisecond. There is no rhyme or reason as to why any innocent person should be confined behind bars and wait years for an actual trial on account of not stemming from an affluent family with boundless resources at their disposal and, secondly, because they are Black. As the great Dr. Martin Luther King Jr. said during the tumultuous sixties, we ought to judge someone based on the content of their character, not the color of their skin.

Upon graduating from The University of West Georgia with a degree in Criminal Justice, I boldly launched my community empowerment career with the penal system, the horrid demise of the Black family. Here, I noticed the disproportionate number of Black men in comparison to their white male counterparts. Also, those who committed white-collar crimes, such as fraud and money laundering, were sprinkled amongst the majority of men charged with blue-collar crimes. Typically committed by those in a lower social class, these crimes range from shoplifting to assault.

While the literate, affluent group worked to manipulate paperwork to their financial benefit, the illiterate ones found themselves behind bars because they failed to read or understand the law. This disproportionate inmate demographic ignited a fire in me to dig deeper. The Bureau of Justice Statistics reported that 75% of state inmates and 59% of federal inmates did not complete high school. Hence, these citizens did not even hold that highly needed high school diploma that people often take for granted. In further research, I discovered a direct correlation between literacy, graduation, and incarceration rates. The main prototype for an inmate was a Black male with an eighth-grade education. Ah ha. This was a defining moment. How could my first book, *From Remedial to Remarkable*, help eradicate this biased epidemic if these middle schoolers read my story before making a life-altering decision that landed them behind bars? Also, by default, this statistic could easily become me, my brother, or my best friends at any routine traffic stop. Just looking at some police officers a certain way or posing a simple question could be reason enough to land a brother behind bars. Where is the promised justice in that?

Before switching gears to a new career field, I must recount the piercing barbwire of a biased penal system fell on my family's headship like a thorny crown. For years, I witnessed my father operate in his love language of providing. No matter the day or season, the fridge was always full, and our home was always warm.

Although my brother and I were first-generation college students, my father and mother covered our first year of tuition. Dad went to work at General Motors and paid the bills like clockwork. He worked full-time in the motor industry, Monday to Friday. Then, he clocked out and worked his driveway mechanic business twenty to thirty hours a week, easily making $50,000 in any given year. So, as you can see, I grew up in a rare, two-parent household. My mother and father worked more than any working man to make an honest wage. Mom was consistently present, caring for my brother and me. We did not lack for anything. I counted my formative years as truly blessed and fortunate because I knew the kid just down the street in a single-mother home, where Mama worked odd jobs and all hours to barely scrape by, with no choice but to leave her little ones to their own devices. I knew about the other poor soul around the bend who came from a family that resorted to selling drugs because of desperation. My family was pretty solid. So, imagine my sheer disbelief when I received the phone call that my very own father was being locked up.

My mouth dropped open as my heart skipped three consecutive beats. How on God's green earth was this even possible? This circumstance was beyond perplexing, as the investigation underscored my father's innocence. Now, the breadwinner of my family, who did not cause harm to anyone, was put under a microscope. Every little action he took was examined at the minutest level. Every motive was questioned as if he had a deceitful agenda. What time did he have to commit a crime when he worked around the clock? He did not even have a speeding ticket to his name. Not even a parking ticket. I was convinced that this was a horrid case of mistaken identity. But the investigation started, and my family felt the blunt end of legal proceedings gone wrong. A year after the prosecution presented their findings, my dad was in court.

To conquer this untimely mountain, my immediate family and I pulled together like a resource-armed brigade. Everyone contributed to legal fees, bond costs, and household affairs. Since the high-profile attorney we hired came with a substantial bill, I voluntarily sold my condominium and motorcycle to make a big dent in the amount due. The first investigation rendered evidence the judge proved to be insufficient. The case was declared a mistrial in Fulton County. Against the odds, Dad came home with us. Our conversations were always limited and short, but he emphatically reminded me of his innocence. Again, we all assumed this chaotic chapter was concluded. This was not so.

Unbelievably, a few short weeks later, the case was picked up by the state of Georgia. This go-around, he was not so lucky. The jury deliberated, and we listened, sitting affixed on pins and needles. Guilty. His attorney's appeal was shot down. My dad started his eighteen-month sentence. How had this nightmare come to pass? I longed to wake up from this traumatic dream. These outcomes were reserved for other people, right? Not for good-hearted, hardworking folks who were just minding their business, trying to put food on the table, and paying bills.

After this gut-wrenching ruling, I immediately tapped into my paid time-off bank. My state employer was now housing the man who led my family to new levels of greatness. I could not enter my workplace and see his daunted face or glean his body caged like a wild animal. Moreover, the inmates who coined me "College Boy" did not need my image tainted. For them, I was the great Black boy of hope. I was a visible emblem that they could dream of reaching higher and achieving better. Never in a million years did I want this positive label to be attached to a supposed crime. It was crucial that I took great precautions in developing into an astute man at the tender age of twenty-five. Becoming another statistic of anything less than ordinary was my archnemesis.

Once my dad was transferred to the county jail, I returned to work for a few months. However, the initial thrill of becoming a leading warden or jail superintendent, infusing these forgotten men with a degree of hope evaporated into thin air. Not only was the time investment absurd, but I also strived to be a part of the solution where young children never ended up in such dismal, shackled predicaments. As soon as I received my teaching offer, I resigned and started a new, more rewarding career. I presumed my encounters with legal investigations ended along with my father's eighteen-month sentence completion. Time would prove me wrong.

In 2009, DeKalb County leaders came under attack. Multiple high-profile leaders were brought under investigation or dragged to court. A year later, the Superintendent, who formerly approved my book sale only two years prior, was indicted. All eyes were on Georgia's fourth largest county, scaling over their financial books with a fine-tooth comb. An anonymous email was sent to the Channel 2 Investigator Report that falsified information about my decisions. The email conveniently and totally negated the thousands of dollars I had donated to local schools or the hundreds of young professionals I had mentored over my many years in leadership in the school district. It only focused on a single book sale. Simultaneously, my adulthood faced another round of ground-shaking legal conundrums.

A year after releasing my first book, the book sale I thought was long put to rest reemerged. This five-figure sales transaction was called into question. History was on replay, but this time, it was me, not my father, in the hot seat. Heads of households who secured leading positions, including me, were under investigation. This was an unsettling, terrifying dilemma that robbed me of my sleep and peace. Fear haunted me like a wicked, green-skinned witch with a maniacal cackle from sunup to sundown. The fear of the unknown was a devil lurking under my college bunk bed, like occasional night terrors during my pledging process. Only this monster was all too real, my friend. Despite this seizing anxiety, I was confident that concluding evidence would point to my innocence. How could it not? I was innocent. Yet, I dutifully followed every step my direct manager conveyed and went through the internal chain of command. In the back of my weary mind, I was reminded of the trauma my family and I were subjected to when my father was unfairly thrown into prison. It was as fresh as the day it happened. There was no justice then. Conscientiously, I worried about justice being rightly served now.

Much like the headlining executives of the county, all men of color, I, too, was deemed guilty until proven innocent. This final ruling would only transpire after two separate investigations coupled with nine months of grueling agony. An in-house exploration amongst DeKalb officials fomented the first tier of the investigation. The paperwork was all in order. Title I executives signed off. After receiving word that their findings confirmed all protocol was followed and no written policy was broken, I was beyond relieved. I held out hope that life would roll out smoothly going forward. Perhaps my old fears had been unfounded. Surely, this would be a district-level mistrial, and all qualms would be put to rest.

To my immense despair, there were two more tiers of investigations taking root, and then I understood this whole conundrum was far from over. The Georgia Professional

Standards Commission and the DeKalb County District Attorney's office were soon to be in receipt of my file. Since my face was plastered on the front page of every statewide newspaper, officials worked to cover their butts. Yet, I was punished beyond measure.

Takeaways – Transactions Are Not Black And White

Investigations are defined as a formal or systematic examination or research. These procedures are to assess the written documentation and verbal authorizations before constructing a definitive conclusion. A series of steps, including the gathering of evidence and analyzing data, in addition to proving proposed theories, must be implemented and, at times, repeated before any charges are made. Reasonable grounds to believe the suspect is guilty of alleged crimes are to occur before the prosecution proceeds to rightfully arrest or convict anyone. Then, a nearly unbiased, selected jury or governing body must find the defendant guilty. In an instant, strangers or former associates hold your very destiny and well-being, and, in my case, my livelihood, in their hands. One hopes that those hands are kind or, at the very least, fair.

Blink and realize that just because everything made sense and was blatantly legal in writing, the outcome can totally ignore these factual letters on the wall. Hence, by people turning a blind eye to proof underscoring a person's innocence, honest lives are demolished like a century-old landmark towering across the city landscape. The fall is painful to witness but even more gruesome to experience. While it is devastating to watch a historic building or statue crumble to its demise, words fail to convey the utter despair and the magnitude of destruction doing likewise to a man's soul. To say I meandered through my days without a constant, assured sense of self or reaffirming purpose is an understatement. My mind reeled. My heart was like a locomotive puffing out one exhausted breath after another as I trekked down the track that had become my life's trajectory. In all the years since my father's incarceration, despite what society would have us believe, nothing had changed. The same prejudices existed that had long been instilled in a certain group of people to regard their fellow human beings as less than instead of equal.

Since these legal actions are typically conducted by a third party, whatever you do, please do not attach your value to their truths. Stand firm on what you claim to be the true depiction of your identity. You know in your deepest recesses who you are and whose you are: a child of God. God sees the heart, while man sees the image crafted by a misguided society. Your name can be thrown in the mud at the drop of a dime, even when you strategically built a cross-generational brand and impactful legacy from the bottom up with immense integrity of blood, sweat, and tears. To that light, I am here to set the record straight and to officially renounce the crooked fallacies recorded in the history books. Yes, I am here to show those exiled by the masses that an untimely delay or demotion cannot eradicate a promised destiny. But first, let us take a gander at the isolated day responsible for making this necessary, one that flipped my world upside down.

"Don't fear the enemy
who attacks you;
fear the fake friend
who hugs you."

Author Unknown

4

The Unlawful Demotion

Acquiring a leadership position is an attractive, although risky, pursuit. It is reserved for brave souls, not the faint of heart. Not everyone has robust gumption running through their marrow to pursue such a lofty goal. By the same token, the bountiful rewards of securing greater influence and income are like a magnetic, golden carrot. For those who have such foresight, initiative, and wherewithal to do so, we hop through hoops, playing politics until the desired role is landed. Yet, leading an organization does not make one immortal or shielded from demotion. No one is above scrutiny. The higher you rise, the shakier the pedestal becomes, especially if it lacks a firm foundation. Even then, you can balance everything right, external forces beyond your control can shatter the empire and legacy you have built. As a case in point, all you need to do is scroll through the morning headlines, and you are bound to find one CEO being demoted or a president being impeached. Although these headships are given a powerful title, there is a board of directors that serves as the checks and balances. For this decision-making group, their ultimate goal is to ensure the elected leader follows the bylaws and projects the organization in the best light.

Attacks on prominent figures hit the smallest organizations to the most profitable business models. For example, two leading figures of Apple, Inc. were two former allies who turned to odds with one another. Behind closed doors, Steve Jobs worked to remove John Sculley as CEO in 1983. In a startling plot twist, the board joined forces with Sculley. Jobs was demoted from his managerial position. A few short months thereafter, he submitted an official letter of resignation. Occasionally, some leaders throw in the white towel of surrender to avoid further scrutiny. They opt to accept the plausible consequences of alleged actions to make the emotional torture cease. Arriving at a point where the final outcome is enacted yields a profound sense of solace. A turning point to bring the risk and reward dichotomy back into alignment with our greater life purpose is a life-saving recourse. Place this wise nugget in your back pocket for the challenging days ensuing.

The inevitable doomsday arrived. My office calendar did not reflect April 1, but I was certain I was being horrifically pranked. As soon as I opened my eyes that morning, I mumbled to myself, "Is this really happening?" This had to be a horrible joke gone wrong. Never in a million years had I fathomed a book I authored would be on trial, but on August 10, 2010, a corporate persecution was commenced. This gloomy morning, my energy was off, but I fulfilled my usual a.m. commitments. Around seven o'clock, I dropped my son off at his elementary school. Before closing the car door, he recited our routine mantra, which I had instilled in him since his toddler years. "Dad, work hard and watch good things happen."

His innocent words uttered from his youthful mouth lanced me. Why did this young man know anyone in our family could still attain greatness despite the wicked ways of the world? Then, I took a deep breath, looked him squarely in the eyes, and forced a smile on my tired face. I chose to flip the narrative running through my head. Although my little guy was simply regurgitating a life approach I preached to him, it was a timely empowerment vitamin. He was right. There was wisdom beyond his few years in those words. "Thank you, son." I watched him scamper toward the school and join the other kids, and then I was off.

As I begrudgingly jumped on I-20 East towards Stone Mountain, Georgia, I took a few profound breaths to remind myself that I was alive, although facing the fight of a lifetime. Heading to the county office off Mountain Industrial Boulevard, my disbelief peaked. Over the course of this thirty-minute ride that seemed to drag on for an eternity, my fear of the unknown became exacerbated. That original vitamin pulverized into thin air. My chest tightened. It felt like I was being buried alive. My chest heaved with each breath. Invisible hands squeezed my heart. Thankfully, I had never experienced a heart attack, but I imagined my reacting organs closely mirrored one. Instead of submerging myself into such debilitating, alarming physical side effects or calling 911, I quickly regrouped. That was the last thing I needed after everything else I had been through! However, I formulated a quick plan to calm my nerves. To ease my anxiety, I phoned my trusted advisor and long-time mentor, Dr. Percy Mack.

At the onset of my educational career years ago, I had the esteemed honor of working under the tutelage of Dr. Mack at a DeKalb County high school. A graduate of Savannah State University, this legendary leader had over forty-two years of experience in the educational field throughout the southeast region of the United States. Dr. Mack was serving as principal of a high school, while I was an assistant principal at the feeder middle school. He amplified an unmatched, perfect blend of exemplary leadership and village-style standards. After watching him establish a winning culture in his school, I decided to model my leadership style after his. What better role model than him? Once he was promoted to Executive Director, he coached me to acquire a principal position at a local high school, just as he had done many years ago.

Fast forward a tenacious decade, Dr. Mack had been nominated as the Superintendent of the Year in 2006 by the National Association of Black School Educators while he operated as Superintendent of Dayton Public Schools. There, he piloted the launch of C.A. Johnson High School Health Sciences Magnet and the Navistar Diesel Technology Program, amongst other notable achievements. Just as he had done in Georgia, he was making a name for himself in another state, giving students the tools to dream outside societal boxes. If anyone could be the voice of reason, it would be this man who I trusted with my personal and professional concerns for years. I hoped and prayed that he would speak words of wisdom and act as one cheering from the sidelines while I ran a starkly different race to the top marathon.

Thankfully, when he read my name on his caller ID, he still picked up. When his fatherly voice answered on the other end of the phone, I breathed out a long sigh of relief. The muscles within my chest cavity untightened, and the built-up tension released through my fingertips, even though I maintained a steady grip on my steering wheel. Careful to keep my eyes straight ahead to safely maneuver through Atlanta's infamous rush hour traffic, I readied myself for a timely, inspirational conversation. It also crossed my whirling mind that having my eyes focused ahead was a fitting metaphor for my current predicament. A steady gaze with my mind's eye on seeing this long journey through and leaping over any further roadblocks was crucial.

On this tumultuous day, I prayed relentlessly like Paul who directed believers two thousand years ago: "Rejoice always, pray without ceasing, give thanks in all circumstances; for this is the will of God in Christ Jesus for you." In retrospect, I know I fought like heavyweight champion Evander Holyfield to knock out self-doubt and tap into my gratitude bank during those unsettling circumstances. Yet, I still needed an earthly voice of comforting reassurance that this, too, would pass. I firmly believe that God often speaks through people, and Dr. Mack was the chosen one I needed. This new, unfamiliar space infringed upon peace like never before as I continued pressing forward. How I longed for that "peace that surpasses all understanding" scripted in the good book of Philippians! Nothing in my training and no one in my inner circle had experienced such a traumatizing paradigm shift, but I knew my mentor would offer appropriate guidance and words of encouragement. I was not disappointed. Dr. Mack offered a futuristic interpretation of this valley from the lens of senior leadership as he stood at the mountaintop of his achievements.

I tuned in to his wise counsel once again. "Simpson, accept the demotion. You will bounce back. Remember, you have the skill set that someone will need along the way."

Nodding my head in quick agreement, I realized he could not observe my gesture. So, I uttered, "Yes, sir. Thank you. I needed to hear that." As per usual, Dr. Mack had conveyed a realistic approach to navigating this hell in an authentic nature. "I knew you were the right one to call in this moment of boiling water," I added. I wiped the sweat beads from my face, feeling as if that pot might boil over.

"Not to worry, Ralph. Glad I could help."

I thanked him profusely again, then ended the call, keeping a tight grip on the steering wheel and my eyes ever ahead.

Renewed with some semblance of career redemption on the horizon, I turned into the DeKalb County School District's parking lot. My mentor had never steered me wrong before, and I trusted his recommendation. As that overused axiom goes, it was time to face the music. I just hoped the music would not blare too loud and start disintegrating all hope. Preferably, a resolute, relaxing melody to the tune of Not Guilty would be perfect. Yet, I knew better than to walk in that overzealous expectation.

After I secured a space front and center at the central office, I straightened my bow tie in the rearview mirror. I flashed myself a dazzling smile, hoping to convince myself that I was ready for this uneventful match. I realized this was not a dream and that a plausible nightmare could very well await beyond those glass entry doors. My posture was to accept the ruling and begin a long-awaited healing process. Mentally, I was beyond drained and in dire need of a positive mental infusion or, better yet, an extended vacation on Belize's beaches. I would deal with whatever consequences presented themselves afterward. The upcoming four hours would go down in my personal history as one of the worst outcomes of my life.

At about 10:00 am., the district-level deliberation began. The Chief Human Resources Officer, our Interim Superintendent, the Deputy Superintendent, the Executive Assistant to the Superintendent, and the Director of Internal Affairs were all seated around the board table facing me. The cold ambiance mirrored a biased courtroom with the judge and jury. All eyes were fixated on me and ready to read out my damning sentence. Although I negated to invite my attorney, I was confident in my ability to strategically navigate this situation, especially since I had previously been enlightened to a brewing demotion.

This life-changing meeting was promptly called to order with the overarching goal of officially demoting me. I could almost hear a gavel echoing through the room and a judge calling the hearing to order. Immediately, I assumed a stance of courage and confidence. As I masked the immense disappointment in a system I had grown to love, I mustered up the energy to mask my emotions and made eye contact with each person, all the while maintaining a blank, serious face.

Once each person rendered their findings and opinions, these key personnel asked if I had any final comments.

Initially, I attempted to mask my frustration and simply said, "No, I am fortunate to still be employed." I intentionally refrained from throwing a biting tone into my voice, but I knew better. I had to take the higher road.

Then, I remembered what Dr. Percy Mack had advised and who I was. I posed this question to the group: "How much time do you have before you retire?"

Each person stated various timeframes, ranging from five to ten years. Their confidence spoke to their satisfaction with being vested and at the top of the hierarchical structures. All the while, I tried not to sneer at their pompous attitudes as they sat safely in their protected positions of authority. Yet still, I suppressed my unbearable angst and swallowed down my pride. It would do me no favors to anger these folks who held my livelihood in their grasp, nor was I in any position to pull any tricks out of my proverbial bag.

Then, one person curiously replied, "Why do you ask?"

Stoically, I leaned forward and said, "I am asking because I want to make sure y'all are around when I come back." There, I said the one thing I could say that would end this detrimental meeting on a high note, ultimately challenging their erroneous verdict. I spoke with an air of confidence, no trace of sarcasm or derision.

You could literally hear my pen stroking my signature on the printed documents. No one spoke or communicated a comeback. Some gaped. A couple awkwardly cleared their throats. All avoided prolonged eye contact. Off the record, I presumed the majority cosigned my shared prophecy and anticipated my rightful return. I would control what I could and would not give them an easy win.

As soon as I finished inking my last John Hancock on the formal paperwork, accepting my demotion, I exited that room with my identity intact and my head held high. The news spread like uncontrollable wildfires during a California drought. By noon, the information was disseminated to all major media outlets. Out of hundreds of achievements worthy of being highlighted over the course of my career, this blemish was now the top story, tarnishing my reputation. Sources stated that a salary-earning executive assistant hand-delivered my images and meeting notes to a big-time reporter. Whether a person was listening to the radio or tuned in to the midday news, it seemed like the entire state of Georgia learned of my now-tainted legacy and coinciding consequences. This is evidence that you can be an honest, hardworking change agent committed to the greater good, yet one decision can flip the odds against you in a matter of moments.

Accepting this unlawful demotion was not an admission of guilt on my part, not by a long shot. No law was broken. No crime was committed. No policy was violated. All heartfelt hopes of inspiring just one more child to fall in love with reading and subscribe to endless possibilities awaiting the resilient person was abruptly met with an unforeseeable, near-death punishment. My acceptance was my outward act of faith, knowing this publicly debilitating situation would never emerge as a death sentence to my burgeoning legacy. No, I would not sit there like I was on death row and accept my lotted fate. I had built my career structure and social network before. I would do so again. In fact, my ability to learn, regroup, and plow ahead would be predicated on the person I saw in the mirror every single morning as I drove to a job, only to serve in a position far beneath my qualifications. In the months that followed, I continued with my life's mission, empowering marginalized groups and improving student outcomes.

In the physical form, I was still alive and going through the motions of being "Simp" to thousands of onlookers. Yet, my faith in humankind, people who looked like me and worked in the educational industry alongside me, was nearing complete extinction. Maybe it was buried and wrapped in layered linens, mummifying the most elite Egyptian royalty from 1400 B.C. Nonetheless, I remembered that I, too, was a resilient king. My mission to increase literacy rates and add to each school's ratings was dismissed. My professional track record and career opportunities I rightfully attained were demolished with a wrecking ball of unwarranted judgment. In those harrowing early days following my unfair demotion, I had to speak truth and faith over the situation as I faced myself in the mirror every morning. Every failure is an opportunity to learn and grow. I would control what I could and leave the rest to God. I refused to be consumed by the trumped-up charges, nor would I play the blame game or seek revenge on those who had pulled the plank out from under me. The higher road extended in front of me. I confidently jumped into my trusty vehicle called Integrity and rode that bumpy highway. The opinions and judgments of others would not define my rightful comeback.

Takeaways - From Ruin To Relief

Life without rain and trials paves out to be a mundane journey. Without some degree of strife, you may forget how strong, gifted, and courageous you are. Between experiences and self-evolution, you will be blindsided by decisions made by humanity, including you. When countless variables are at play, it is easy to become absorbed by an isolated event. However, after sufficient time and possibly counseling, choose to bravely step beyond that initial shock factor. If you remain planted in a sea of confusing misery, you may waste away in complacency and remorse. The key is to stay true to who you are and know your side of the story matters. Learn from your missteps and move forward.

Now, it was time to become a visible emblem of a resilient man determined to rise from the ashes like a blessed phoenix and reclaim his rightful throne. But first, I channeled any remaining confidence, dripping slowly into my vein like an IV given to a person in intensive care. When a glimmer of energy reverberated throughout my body, it was time to arduously dig myself out of this suffocating rabbit hole. I held my trusty shovel of hard work, slowly starting the digging process. The proverbial light at the end of the tunnel grew brighter every time I planted the spade into the soil. With each spoon of gathered earth, I threw it along with defeat over my shoulder. I intentionally removed untrue dirt splatters that tarnished my reputation. Until I unearthed my transformative brand and renewed spirit, I would fight like my life depended on it.

Everyone starts out as a baby, a blank slate, a ball of potential. Although December 14 marked the beginning of my life on this earth, I must recognize another that transpired on August 10, 2010. To some degree, this summer date marked the inception of my rebirth. Yes, I was still Lil Simp, the student who played park baseball and rose to ROTC captain. I was still the struggling high school student who went from taking remedial courses to a soaring man with a doctorate degree under his belt. Out of twenty-plus first cousins, I reminded myself that I was the great hope in my family's lineage, the only one to attain such academic and professional successes. The young professional that Danny

Buggs, a former NFL player and public school administrator, spoke greatness into one Saturday afternoon was me. These truths anchored me in some timely hope. Notwithstanding, this life-altering debacle was not a period to the legacy I was crafting but simply a comma, a symbol of a new arising. Ironically, the weight of the world lessened with each step I took toward my car that fateful day. It was time to dig deep and find the motivation to rebuild, as my name was still being smeared and my character assassinated. Yet, I made the conscious decision to ignore partial acts of character defamation and instead invest my energy into what was within my grasp: my daily actions. I would be like a phoenix rising from the ashes or the new vegetal growth after one of those all-consuming forest fires. Yet, I cleaved to a few mustard seeds of faith that God was pruning me for a greater season. Wisdom taught me that I would never be the same man after being ripped into shreds and hung to dry on public display.

"Don't believe everything
you hear.
Real eyes realize
real lies."

Tupac Shakur,
American Rapper and Actor

FROM DEMOTION TO PROMOTION

DR. RALPH L. SIMPSON

5

Simp vs. The Opinion

Being in the public limelight requires a highly revered leader to live higher, often impossible norms. Staggering standards of exceptional excellence put such individuals in a league of their own if and when they are able to attain such glory. This level of attention is garnered by people who opt for the above-average lifestyle. To be sure, this demanding lifestyle is not for the faint of heart. Yet, when glorious times are experienced, that blessed light magnifies each winning characteristic and good deed. Like every facet of life, there is a distressing flip side to that costly coin. When the limelight is shined upon a human error that the public frowns upon, the formerly distinguished light transforms into a raging, all-consuming fire. The damage it leaves in its wake takes exorbitant effort and time to clean up. Even when the slate is wiped clean, you are starting below ground zero but with an unforgiving, weighted monkey wrapped tightly around your back. Too often, a mass-scale choir of fans throwing up pom poms cheering for your victory can quickly transform into opinionated doubters aiming daggers at you. Such swift, polarizing behaviors in a person's disposition only multiply the pain of being torn to pieces on a national platform. A formerly successful person is massively abandoned, leaving him or her with boiling burn marks and a scorched spirit. Anyone born under the earthly sun is a human being at risk of falling from stardom faster than a strike of lightning. That severed, shaky ground erupts quickly, and profound pain is unimaginable. At the inception of their above-average journey, this individual transformed into an action-taking leader, deciding to move past mediocrity or any systemic restraint.

Often, young boys are frequently bred to be team players and play sports. Extracurricular activities such as these build a student's grit, well-being, social-emotional growth, and more. When I looked into my son's eyes, I personally saw a genius, nearly a Jackie Robinson replica. In fact, when my son was three years old, we strolled to the equipment section in Target. I advised him to choose any bat he wanted. His curious eyes scanted across the shelf a few times before he grabbed a bat nearly twice his size. With both hands, he wrapped his fingers tightly around the handle like a true MVP of Tee Ball. Then, he eyed the cheerful cashier standing at his metaphoric home plate and dragged it to the checkout counter. It was time to show him the baseball rules I learned, exposing him to a less-traveled world of sports.

Running 440 yards around school tracks for countless hours each week extends far beyond the goal of a child releasing anxious, trapped energy. Such physical exertion also acts as a mental buffer to any doubt challenging an aspiring professional sports player's grandiose dream. Operating in the space of student-athlete is preached as a necessary function, but too often, academic proficiency comes second to sports in disadvantaged households. Test scores, public policies, and programs cunningly convince marginalized children that they are less smart than their racial counterparts.

Simply scan the latest rankings on GreatSchools.org. Within moments, one will find a disproportionate number of students graduating from school but lacking college preparedness or student experience within a schoolhouse heavily committed to closing achievement gaps. Dig deeper and find confirming evidence underscoring the two strikes against these gifted children. Such school districts have a seesaw illustration where schools in more affluent areas mold education and sports as one, while those in the lower socio-economic brackets are heavily inundated with less-than-average academic excellence. Unfortunately, at such an impressionable age, it seems these brilliant minds are routinely entangled by life-changing bars of limited success.

From my purview, African American males often strive to excel at sports with hopes of securing a multi-million-dollar contract in professional basketball or football, a sure golden ticket to their family's financial freedom and rise from poverty and desperate desolate life in some cases. These chosen boys must be the first to champion a full-circle cause with humble pride. Michael Vick is one prime example of this hopeful trajectory. Stemming from a two-parent household like me and 70% of children in the US, Vick was the proud son of a sandblaster and a devout mother. Vick realized his parents' aim for his academic achievement in a drug-ridden community. After his graduation, he turned down a full ride to Syracuse University and matriculated to Virginia Tech. Here, his family's legacy would scale to new heights. In 2001, at the inception of the 21st century, his professional football career catapulted when he was drafted by the Atlanta Falcons. This genesis marked the beginning of a six-year, sixty-two-million-dollar contract. Regrettably, Vick's quest to win a Super Bowl Championship with his team was shattered to a million pieces.

Barely over the average age of a college graduate, Vick's young adult life hit a perilous occasion. His burgeoning legacy was publicly intertwined with a dog-fighting scandal in 2007. Initially, he fearfully denied all associations with the crime, one prevalent activity in his hometown. Eventually, Vick listened to his legal counsel and pled guilty. He was sentenced to twenty-three months in prison plus one million dollars in restitution. As a former dog owner, I do not condone the harsh treatment of any mammal, canines and humans included. By the same token, I do believe that punishment should fit the crime. Michael Vick was a first-time offender, a community leader, and an all-star. Perhaps weekly community service and a hefty fine would have been more fit for his shunned hobby. Here is my case in point. All you need to do is spin the globe. Watch your fingers land on a random country where dogfighting is still garnering Colosseum-level crowds. Such competitions continue to be a hallmark for revenue streams and leisure activities in multiple countries. From Afghanistan to Japan to Russia, the betting sport stemming from war times between Britain and Rome in 43 A.D. still prevails today in lieu of animal protection agencies' efforts or enacted laws.

According to Wayne Pacelle, former president of the Humane Society of the USA, our great nation is still guilty of dog fighting. Animal cruelty is prevalent and leveraged as a means of generating profit for circuses and zoos alike. Are not all mammals created equally and rightful recipients of equitable treatment? In addition, it is estimated that 40,000 people within the borders of this great nation still participate in this bloody, vicious sport, yet they remain free to live their lives as law-abiding citizens. Here, it is evident that leaders who stand in the limelight are held to a taller order, almost impossible standards of perfection, than the average person.

Much like Michael Vick, I, too, was the sacrificial lamb, an emblem of what not to do when drafted for a top-tier, leading position. One motive behind this illuminated chastisement is to benefit the common good. Speaking of sacrificial lamb, that term often describes Jesus Christ's opposition. Unexpectedly, the people who celebrated his triumphal entry into Jerusalem by waving palm branches a week earlier were the same ones who demanded his crucifixion. The unsettling aspect of public punishment is that the castigation extends far beyond the penalty imposed. At a time when I needed my support group the most, friends and colleagues started deserting me as if I was a villainized castaway. From their unaware lens, I was a running man on contagious fire with a county-wide target on my back. Fear paralyzed them from running alongside me to comfortingly throw a fire-retardant, water-drenched blanket around my shoulders to smother and mute the flames. It is a sad realization what an immobilizing motivator fear can be, often for divisive, counterproductive reasons.

Years later, a small group of associates confessed that they quickly established distance for their own protection. In a vulnerable dialogue admitting the possession of skeletons in their closet, they fearfully imagined what the county would do to them after witnessing my persecution. When the limelight is shining on the supposedly guilty, devastating sins of all onlookers may be deathly exposed. Suddenly, it is every man for himself. Self-preservation and popular opinion quickly take precedence over being your brother's keeper.

From 6:00 in the morning to 11:00 at night, my alleged book scandal was breaking news across media platforms, including Fox 5 Atlanta and WSBTV-Channel 2. Although scandal is a popular buzzword that garners massive attention, it is also an equally damaging noun when attached to anyone's reputation. Webster defines scandal as an act or event that is morally or legally wrong and causes public outrage. Take a quick gander at the United States presidents from 1990 to 2020. Only two of the five elected presidents successfully left office without an alleged or proven scandal attached to their legacy, Barack Obama and possibly George Bush. No one ever lost their presiding office. Shockingly, mounting evidence showed some incidences done behind closed doors were quite heavily laced in turpitude. Contrarily, my defining book transaction was done in plain sight. Every step of the process was legally sound, backed by official paperwork and executive signatures. The funds to purchase the books were only released because a dozen colleagues and I found this common exchange legitimate. Furthermore, full restitution was made from all sales.

Government entities purchase books all the time. Such agreements go left field when the court of public opinion catches wind of any event smeared with lies. They quickly sentence the defendant to damnation. The great news is that even within this abyss of capitalistic thinking and misconstrued information, a special few remained loyal like clockwork. One of my closest friends consistently corrected any circulating false narratives he overheard. When an ill-informed person finished recounting their pieced-together narrative, he would lean over and say, "Listen, Simpson would not steal candy from a baby. The man followed protocol but fit the prototype for the blame guy." Upon hearing him share this anecdote, I was comforted to learn a few soldiers were in the streets cutting down rumors in an instant. While rumor mills continued to pollute metro-Atlanta sound waves like an overplayed scratched record, I suited up for my new role. First and foremost, I was still a free man and committed to being a provider.

Once I hit 285 East to head to my newly assigned workplace, I switched my iPod to Tupac's greatest hits. "Me Against the World" boomed over my Bose speakers as I nodded my head to its inspiring beat. Then, my ears tuned in deeper as he suggested, "Don't settle for less; even the genius asks questions. Be grateful for blessings. Don't ever change. Keep your essence." His lexicon selection heavily resonated with me as I embarked upon this new season. No, I was not dodging lethal bullets in a gang war on street corners, but I was dodging verbal warfare in the press. Although this new life was synonymous with a pressurized gas chamber, I chose to stay ten toes down and do my best. From the depths of my suffocating soul, I knew that I was a fighter and survivor. Men and leaders alike were never made overnight. A glimmer of hope struck my heart as I reminded myself that my legendary comeback would not be an overnight phenomenon either.

During my first week at Troy High School, I was welcomed with open arms and an air of condolences. Teachers and students assessed my freshly pressed, tailored suit, then offered a candid smile. All that said, however, within a few days, I noticed roadblocks and cold shoulders mounting up throughout the schoolhouse. I was beyond baffled. What on God's green earth was going on? What important memo had I missed? Then, another teacher furiously marched to the principal's office and reported his colleague's uncouth behaviors. To my utter dismay, the unfavorable opinion about yours truly dominating metro-Atlanta influenced one educator to be yet another unnecessary antagonist. This short-sighted pessimist assumed the role of devil's advocate. He carved out a few hours of his time to make the false news a real depiction of me. Although this was not a standards-based activity, this judgmental teacher made one hundred copies of the *Atlanta Journal-Constitution* article, conveying a false narrative about me. Then, full of zeal and himself, he distributed it to his students and anyone else walking down the hall. While he could have been exhausting his eight-hour workday to serve the students and staff at that institution, apparently, he found his irreplaceable hours more valuable to be spent taking someone else down.

Looking back on that unfortunate incident, it is easy to see that his behavior spoke volumes about his character rather than my chalked-up booked scandal. His petty act amplified his inner envy more than the publicized falsities he spread as if he were a contracted news anchor. At any interval, a juicy story took front and center stage. It is a depressing testament to how easily an entertaining story distracts us from any glimmer of legitimacy. That our first instinct is not to sincerely question the validity of such proposed narratives is unfortunate. But that is what sells. Perhaps he had a grave concern for the untruths tainting my character, but based on his tactic, it is more likely that he simply wanted a smear campaign. Moreover, his tasteless approach was divisively unprofessional. I assumed an unbothered posture. I would not be moved. I had already fallen from grace, removed from my proverbial throne. There would be no double jeopardy here. What additional damage could this singular naysayer do? No living soul could impose a horrid personality on me. This teacher's spiteful actions were laughable.

I expressed to the reporting teacher, "I am not upset and have already been through hell. I am good." As the last word echoed from my mouth, I instantly reminded myself that I was assigned to this specific schoolhouse during this special season to make a significant impact. So, I chuckled inside at this unfruitful hurdle, then put another attempted assassination of my recovering reputation to rest.

In the coming weeks, a schoolwide assembly placed the microphone right in my ready hand. Finally, the hour to right the wrongs pouring down on me like a monsoon and threatening to wash me away like a flash flood presented itself. I undoubtedly won the crowd over with my authentic character within ten minutes. Being real with people has always been at the forefront of my mind and methodology. I can spot a faker within minutes of meeting them. Even if someone has charisma and can play the false narrative game for a while, in time, the truth always comes out. Then, the prime-time season to transform my tragic mess into a transformative message, displayed itself. The senior class, who affectionately called me Bow Tie, voted to make me their pre-commencement speaker. Speaking to the high school graduating class would recharge my energy backpack. Their young, pliable minds would soak up the words of wisdom I had to offer. Watching their minds expand as the simple factors of success rolled off my tongue, I surmised my messaging to be more effective and meaningful as a result of my time deep within traumatizing valleys.

When graduation day came, as I looked into the eyes of three-hundred and seventy scholars dressed in their caps and gowns, I recalled my final high school days. After a few remedial courses and uncapped resilience, I, too, had achieved that milestone. I charged the graduates to work hard until they acquired their best possible life. Their souls craved the wisdom I shared as a person who fell from a high place without permanently losing my ultimate sense of self. If I had only experienced mountaintops, my words wouldn't have had the impact they did. I told these youths that they would go through ups and downs throughout life and reminded them that, even when standing at the pinnacle of success, they should not look down on others. There would be people in their lives who would be stepping stones to their achievements. Others would be stumbling blocks, but taken together, those people (or metaphorical stones) would form the path they trod. Taken together, that was life. I wanted them to have enough of a positive outlook to keep dreaming, yet I desired that they also keep their feet rooted to the solid ground as hopeful realists, not destructive pessimists. Like I shared with them, a temporary setback is not a permanent stop sign to your envisioned destination. My greatest hope was that each avid listener would hold their psychological well-being as paramount to the opinionated masses. No longer was I an eyesore to this high school. No, I was a testament to courageously thriving daily when in the eye of a tumultuous storm.

Takeaway – Count Your Opinion First

Mental toughness is single-handedly the needed bulletproof vest when living in a highly opinionated world. Operate under the guise of a growth mindset and remain steadfast in your self-belief. At any moment, you stand toe to toe with an entity attempting to dismantle the core of your essence. Times of turbulent adversity produce greater leadership competencies in comparison to mundane occurrences. Friction resulting from contrasting forces equates to a highly compounded pressure that breaks down nonproductive systems, such as bogus legal processes and judication. Novel tests are present in every facet of life. Such challenges allow you to reconfirm your commitment to your calling and wade in the storm. Acing life's exams requires an unwavering commitment to who you are and where you are going. Just like you study to prepare for a crucial exam, you must put in the hard work in preparation for the sizeable challenges life throws your way.

Dress for where you're going, not for irrelevant opinions on how good you look superficially on the outside. I am a firm believer that people meet your potential by the clothes you wear before they completely trust your leadership ability. First impressions matter. People typically judge the shell of you they see before your innate talents. Although they say you should never judge a book by its cover, people do. Sure, it was gratifying to peer out into the graduating class and see the sea of bow ties peeking above their gowns. This symbolized that the opinions of people who matter are a much better gauge of your positive work.

An Ethiopian proverb advises, "An elephant does not limp when he is walking on thorns." While dropping your head and tiptoeing on eggshells may be a natural proclivity to unpredictable attacks, fight that temptation with every ounce of self-respect you have. Walk proud, shoulders back and head held high, like a three-ton elephant dominating the Saharan Desert by its presence alone. Cleave to the self-image you know to be true. Failures, both in the personal mirror and the public arena, are temporary reminders of your blind spots (we all have them). They are not equipped to derail your destiny train from its tracks. Pervasively refuse to be consumed by defeat. Do not trip on a few missteps your human nature exposed you to commit. Transform stress-laced scenarios into legacy-changing outcomes. Your next destination will provide the rationale and needed answers to former tests.

Lean into your authentic life purpose, the one planted at your core before you knew what an opinion actually was. Remold those statements as signs of admiration regardless of the original intent. Iconic figureheads hundreds grew to admirably love can morph into burning flames at any instant. Let that flow like water off your shoulders. Persevere and perform as your better self. Start small. Gain momentum. Make people remember your name.

"Everybody's dealing with and going through something. It's how you deal with it and continue to move forward that determines your destination."

Deion L. Sanders,
Former NFL Player and College Football Coach

FROM DEMOTION TO PROMOTION

DR. RALPH L. SIMPSON

6

The Costly Persecution

Media can be extremely persuasive in an everyday, average person's life. There is what is reported, and then there is what is documented, most likely closest to the actual truth. This supposed truth can blindly convince viewers there is a 0% chance of precipitation in the middle of spring in Georgia. It is sadly amazing what people will believe in certain circumstances. Even when they have nothing to gain from such beliefs, sometimes deception plays a more powerful role than truth. It is easier to be blind, even when facts present themselves before crowds. But so, despite a strong spirit of discernment urging a person to grab an umbrella from their trunk, this impressionable professional leaves the parking lot without it, thinking they have their facts right. Then, boom, the heavens open, leaving all walkers soaked because they failed to do their own due diligence to personally research weather trends in surrounding cities. From a humanistic perspective, you are guilty as soon as your image is plastered across every morning edition's front page. People rarely do necessary, valid research to arrive at their own conclusions. It is far easier to form an uninformed opinion on any matter than to seek facts at any cost.

The First Amendment of the Constitution granted license for entities to freely express their opinions, unrestricted by biased government censures. Such freedom speaks to the massive privileges of living in our proclaimed free world, this great nation. In that same vein, flip our proverbial coin: such liberties can infringe upon an innocent person's right to pursue the American dream absent to the pressure of being under a hypercritical microscope meant to examine every minute imperfection, then exploit it at their own whims. Today, new laws have been enacted to loosely control the potential excessive emotional damage a social media post or poorly written newspaper article, meaning factual content, can cause to a law-abiding citizen minding his or her own business. However, most regrettably, these laws often fail to deliver the very protections they were enforced to do.

Millions witness the rapid pace at which an act of public persecution writes an all-access pass that permits multi-dimensional rejection. At an interruptive juncture, it appears like your feet are cemented under a never-ceasing rain cloud, slowly drowning you mentally, physically, spiritually, and even financially. How can you regain your solid footing under these circumstances? What buoys your resolve? No doubt, such agonizing suffering reflects those moments not voluntarily disclosed to the masses, but it definitely warrants genuine empathy. Stepping into another's shoes may open a compassionate door that offers better understanding, new insight, or financial mercy.

Financial woes are a surefire way to send any dependable person into a deep depressive state or clouded judgment, which leads to a petrifying somersault off the invisible Twin Towers. According to United States courts, over 350,000 Americans leverage bankruptcy to escape a fiscally deconstructive hurricane. Whether a person files Chapter 7 or Chapter 13, these legal proceedings tank credit scores and new asset acquisitions seven to ten years following. That is a high price demanded. Declaring bankruptcy fails to wipe one's slate completely or gift a free pass to spend frivolously. Contrarily, amid devastating financial hardships, starting over from scratch seems more advantageous and sometimes a person's only way forward. A single act of substantial debt relief serves as the last Hail Mary to regain any semblance of sound financial peace. Yet, judgment does not stop there. Anyone who pursues this legal matter opens their world to outsider conviction and persecution, which come with their own high prices.

Constant inflation sends the cost of living through already leaky roofs. Shaky foundations threaten to crumble apart, a person's whole structure going down. These structures could be our livelihoods, reputations, or legacies. Meanwhile, creditors and lenders will hold this dreaded resolution against new and loyal customers alike for many decades. Given these inevitable, most unfortunate outcomes, living above the poverty line evolves into a key objective for one's mental well-being and overall livelihood.

On the first and fifteenth of every month, my bank account coldly, heartlessly reminded me that this costly persecution could have driven me, like many poor souls before, to a similar desperate state. However, I made lifestyle adjustments with haste once I accepted my demotion. I kept my dignity in check. Eyes and heart forward, I marched onward, against threatening odds. I took an inventory of what I owned and adjusted my spending habits. Next, I started liquidating tangible assets and modes of transportation. I had already bid farewell to my Suzuki motorcycle a few years prior. I was maturing as a father to two amazing children now, so the adrenaline rush I got in my younger glory days from speeding down open highways came with less exhilaration.

There was no possible solution to immediately make ends meet. My bills far outweighed my monthly income. I pulled the lever and filed for bankruptcy. No possession was too smooth to sacrifice paying child support or my mortgage. Mini Cooper, BMW 750, and a few other debts were gone. By my liquidation process's closure, I had one remaining asset: my three-story home.

Frankly, after suffering a consecutive $50,000 pay cut over three years, that item and a new vehicle were all I needed. So, I hit the dealership before the bankruptcy dinged my credit score. I grabbed a certified, used BMW X5. Filing for bankruptcy was the responsible reset. Unfortunately, invasive monetary ramifications did not halt there.

Being in an executive leadership role comes with its perks, such as one's ability to transform a school region or earn a six-figure salary. In that same light, watching my father earn thousands in our driveway after his nine-to-five with General Motors proved advantageous for our entire family. After a few remedial courses, I matriculated to senior year, becoming the driver of a 1980 shiny, Spelman-blue Camaro, compliments of a hardworking father. I was the talk of town when I personalized my ride with a spoiler, tinted windows, a sound system, and custom wheels. More importantly, his industrious, resourceful example also taught me a few life lessons.

First, never let your right hand know what your left hand is doing. What is done outside of an official workday is separate from what is done off the clock. Do not allow overlap with these separate income-generating worlds. Second, never depend on one income source alone. With numerous uncontrollable variables in our economy and workplaces, it is only wise to have a legitimate side hustle. For yours truly, this was none other than my official business, Rem2Rem LLC, registered with its own employee identification number, totally detached from my Social Security number.

To my utter, horrific surprise, news outlets also tainted my hard-earned brand, spurring a deepening level of raw rejection. Four long years would pass before I would fulfill another book order. Those years felt like decades, like serving a prison sentence when innocent, each day drawn out, wondering when respite would come. It seemed as if my first literary work carried an unmerited scarlet letter, symbolizing a dishonorable discharge from a top-tier position. Listening to gut instinct's counsel, I quickly began distancing myself from certain entrepreneurship ventures, a survival necessity. The termination letters I had received for speaking at prestigious engagements in surrounding areas matched this decision. These rejections bulleted me like I stood in front of a firing squad, pronounced guilty before I had a fighting chance. I projected this great loss since anyone who watched news stations in metro-Atlanta learned about my supposed questionable accusations. However, I was blindsided when I received a politically correct pink slip from notable organizations where I had secured part-time jobs. Would this be the final nail in an invisible coffin that I found myself buried in?

Fervently operating as an authentic, frontline leader in lieu of a job title change remained a professional commitment. As I worked laboriously reinventing and rebranding myself, formerly established cash flow streams consistently transformed into a worsening drought caused by a damning verdict I never deserved. Onlookers would wrongly conclude that I pivoted unscathed without a drastic loss of momentum. To external eyes, I probably appeared bulletproof or immortal, some superhero or deity. Such assumptions people drew all over again although they lacked all the necessary information. Observing my purposeful pace or freshly pressed suit made it appear like I bore this burden with graceful ease. That is not true at all. Since work, family, and life routines were comfortably cruising right along on autopilot before this fabricated scandal, I still moved with the same sense of urgency and purpose, meeting every personal obligation with tact and grace despite harrowing conditions all around me.

In this same vein, acknowledging mounting income restrictions hanging precariously from a thread overhead multiplied into all-too-familiar sleepless nights, but I persisted, nonetheless. I painstakingly worked by channeling unbothered, unbought spirits of civil rights activists, like Xernona Clayton, former vice president of Turner Broadcasting and a Tennessee State University alumnus. Despite staggering rates of both racism and sexism, this African American woman continues to stand on the frontline, sacrificing her life so that, invariably, people like me may progress into a more equitable, brighter future than what she lived. She operated as a virtuous exemplar of her favorite quote: "If you cannot change people around you, change the people around you." Operating at this level filled with much gracious thinking, I decided to change disruptive inputs into my day-to-day life by substituting them with small-step empowering actions I could easily take.

I distanced myself from untrue commentaries. For example, if I was grabbing groceries one sunny afternoon, I avoided glancing over Sunday's newspaper columns. Seeing such blasphemous articles only conjured up yet another gut-punching blow when a familiar face, mine, covered the front-page news. If news stories led the masses to believe that I was that day's hot topic once again, I pressed the power button on my remote control faster than a single blink. I zoomed away from that horrific territory in 0.6 seconds. No longer would I willingly be entrenched in a seemingly bottomless abyss filled with fallacies, lies, or any ugliness. I opted to wrap bitter, wayward thoughts in a gracious, forgiving spirit.

Thankfully, I was legally covered during this whole messy, unfair ordeal. God's grace still interceded on my behalf. As a member of the entity that represents Georgia educators, I was afforded legal representation. Without this timely benefit, a high-quality attorney could have cost me anywhere upwards of $25,000. Although legal dealings persisted for about a year, I was never forced into tapping into nearly depleted savings. This small win reignited my hope flame. Maybe that phoenix would rise from the ashes after all. Mentally, I took a strong stand, then pivoted.

On any given day, you would find me taking a long, heart-racing run down Cascade Road or pumping all the best hits of Biggie Smalls or Tupac. My heart beating with those lyrical beats, feet thudding on the pavement with animated rhythm, I breathed in the fresh air, day after day, pressing forward, onward, and upward. Aiming to invest every ounce of energy into restoring my credibility while maximizing earning potential with the remaining forty hours after allocating the first sixty hours to my main job at school, I reimagined a new trajectory. I am the author extraordinaire of Simpson's story. Even if I had a pen pressed firmly between nimble fingers, forgoing this venture alone, I would take it. Any open road is worth such a risk.

As an assistant principal, I leveraged my ability to still infect change and coast along with it. I yielded to the current leadership, reassuring the present principal, a leader I formerly advised and placed in that position, that I was only there in a supporting role. In stark contrast to decisive people whispering divisive lies in his ears, I had zero interest in stealing his position. Unbeknownst to him and other colleagues, determination to maximize this season that presented a drastic reduction in responsibilities seized me. I literally moved from supervising twenty elementary, middle, high, alternative, charter, and technical schools to collaboratively managing just one. I could efficiently execute this job with my eyes closed. Given this increase in free time, I set my mind on regaining financial footing and securing other income streams.

As if past ripple effects since that dismal day in August were not enough, more restrictive punishments would ensue. Perusing my emails, my tired eyes paused on one that read URGENT. Since I had partnered with this prestigious university as an adjunct professor for three years, I presumed such an email included spring course offerings and schedule options. Would I lecture Organizational Communications or Educational Leadership? I forecasted a student body ready to learn the law and power of restorative practices. Instead, when I opened that message, it read, "Thank you for your notable tenure with our school. After careful consideration, our leaders have decided to go in a different direction with professor selection." This daunting decision shook me at my core, severing an additional twenty-thousand dollars off my annual income. Where rested any loyalty? How could this happen? Questions streamed through my brain matter like a relentless train intent on running me over, stealing hope, and sealing fate. Sweat beaded on skin. Nerves frayed. Impossibility reigned that dismal day.

To my alarm, further destruction darkened my doorstep. Less than a month later, I noticed the scholarship organization I partnered with one time would soon have their weeklong application review. However, I had yet to receive any logistics or travel arrangements. To get ahead of any burgeoning budgetary cuts, I phoned the key contact person. Once I introduced myself, in a computerized tone, the director said, "Dr. Simpson, we are extremely grateful for your two years of service as a reader for the Millenium Scholarship Program. This year, we have finalized our readers' selection and will not need your services." Deflated, I replied, "I do understand. Thank you for your time." He knocked the wind from me. Once I hit "end call" on my phone, I froze, stunned in disbelief. Sure, the $1,000 stipend provided means for adding a tailored suit or two to my timeless collection. Yet, my role with this organization was easily ten times bigger. Not only had my attempt to lessen literary challenges hit a roadblock, but my heartfelt commitment to helping students of color attain college degrees did as well. Each year, I played an instrumental role in aiding those from lower socioeconomic households, as evidenced by their eligibility for the Pell Grant, to secure a full ride to their choice college. Imagine the foregone gratification I experienced again when another societal resolve came to an egregious halt as well. I lost again.

I unplugged, pressing the reset button again. Damn, hell has no fury like a person publicly scorned. I sounded like a broken record player saying, even thinking that. A human being rejected by the masses could literally be doomed forever. If I had learned anything from life's lessons, I understood that I had to take good with bad. Maybe I needed time to seek a new group that could offer impactful opportunities. I seriously pondered this proposed suggestion after suffering this third strike. How much bad luck could a guy take after all? I desperately needed to rewrite the rules of engagement and restock my professional toolbox with better, more powerful tools.

After plowing through official certification options matching my background, I landed on becoming a certified mediator. I had a natural disposition to remain neutral during hostile scenarios and heated debates. By meditating on situations, I would employ a cost-savings resolution for opposing parties, lessening the likelihood they would drive themselves into deeper debt. Game on. I swiped my debit card, then paid $1200 to enroll in the best program starting soonest. Looking at my already demanding schedule, I resumed my student role by carving out two hours after work to master mediation's more profound intricacies. Upon completion of an intensive forty-hour credit course, I passed Georgia's certification exam with 70% or higher. The exact score escapes memory, but since I received approval to apply, I am certain I met the benchmark. I stood one step away from supplementing my current income with a few extra thousand dollars.

With forecasted goals on the back burner, I happily applied to the courts for the final seal of approval. Ecstasy overflowed as I re-engaged tools and strategies I garnered during college and my experience solving conflicts with students, staff, or parents. DENIED. You got to be kidding me. Another denied opportunity was based on an action, not a crime. I already paid in more ways than one can imagine. Knowing a denial is not a permanent no, I exercised my right to appeal the decision to the superior court judge. DENIED. Shaking my head in utter disbelief, I closed that case.

At sunset, neither television nor newspapers were a desirable source for knowing about world affairs. Just seeing a familiar reporter's face conjured a fateful reminder: my persecution had not reached its expiration date. Inwardly, this public torture cost much peace. My pride died. My ego withered. One single action's implications were like awful hazing. But I endured constant, exacerbating mental toil. From brain fatigue to mental agony, such a single-book transaction with its consequences were on constant replay, matching sunrise after sunrise. It was eating me alive. Any past attempts to rebuild my financial structure and professional momentum proved unfruitful. However, I pondered the game of baseball. A major league professional is considered a winning top-tier player if he hits only 30% of pitched balls. Among basic numbers, such low batting averages are automatically deemed a failure. Hence, I needed to retrain, return to home plate, and keep swinging the bat at well-deserved professional opportunities.

Batter up! Home of the Braves, City of Atlanta, here I come. Obstacles were excessively thrown faster than Richard "Cannonball" Redding's blazing-fast pitch. Despite being labeled illiterate, Redding still attended Morris Brown College in his hometown, Atlanta. The Major League Baseball Organization denied him entry. Why? His God-given skin color. Yet, he flipped this rejection into an impetus to make an illustrious history with the Negro Baseball League during the early 1900s. This two-hundred-pound heavy hitter literally struck out Babe Ruth three times on nine pitches. At his career's peak, he was forcibly drafted by the US military. I would consider such a career interruption the worst form of demotion. If Redding could build a notable legacy in lieu of these challenges, then why should I accept any defeat?

Surely, I could flip any flawed reputation demise into a new legacy maker's victory. I perused administrative job openings within the Atlanta Public Schools district. Then bam! A brand-new, state-of-the-art academic facility with an all-male student body right in Atlanta's heart that would bring life's purpose full circle: Best Academy. Nestled in Zone 1, this area was branded as a violence and drugs hub off Donald Lee Hollowell Parkway. My formative years transpired within our family home just five miles from this new school. Irony or perfect timing? As expected, the first-round interview was a homerun. I successfully advanced to the final round, then struck out. Comparatively, two other finalists only accomplished half the career wins and qualifications. The piercing, resounding strike remained a scarlet letter stamped on my educator's certificate, reading: "Pending Investigation." Another shot at redeeming a fraction of my salary loss, maybe $15k, was obliterated again.

Even after serving as an AP at Troy High for nearly a year, my certificate remained under investigation by the Professional Standards Commission. No news is only good news when your livelihood is not hanging in the balance. Why the hold-up? All evidence pointing to my innocence stood clearly in black and white. Unwilling to let the school year end with a certificate undetermined, I phoned my attorney, requesting his assistance. Initially, he discovered the PSC recommended a year-long suspension. Wait a minute, I've had employees charged and found guilty of DUIs remain employed. What was going on? My attorney and I submitted an appeal, requesting a reduction to a thirty-day suspension without pay. After careful, consistent negotiations, the PSC rendered their final judgment of a ten-day suspension. To make matters worse and as a part of the demotion, the school district ordered me to refund the sales transaction's exact amount, $9600. I could never forget that restitution amount, as it far exceeded my new monthly income. The school kept possession of these books, so perhaps, even if by a long shot, my initial mission to elevate literacy amongst disenfranchised groups remained at work. So, I paid the restitution, internalizing that penalty with a slightly satisfied degree. Such financial persecution culminated during the summer with a ten-day unpaid leave consequence.

As I spent days off attending my son's baseball league games, I found reasons for gratitude. These ramifications materialized into a personal nightmare as if my two money-generating hands had been nailed to a blitheful, pitiful cross of restricted cash flow. My gut instinct told me if I endured these setbacks, those around me might feel residual effects. I repositioned my focus on how this fiasco impacted those I loved. As usual, shielding them from judgmental daggers and keeping them close at every chance remained a top priority.

Being anchored by my immediate family provided rich emotional deposits my soul demanded. After public lashing and daily lynchings, my soul grew beyond weary. No onlookers noticed my inner strife, but Mom could sense something wrong. Her restless soul watched her son's reputation be nailed to a casket of lies. Maternal instinct is wild. Each night before her head touched her pillow, she phoned me. Her direct, five-minute call was not to interrogate me or gain some understanding of why these false accusations about her baby boy dominated the city's airwaves. For Mom, she needed me to know she stood in my corner, and this too, would pass. No one ever wants a loving parent to bear anything based on innocent but publicly ridiculed decisions. Talk about shame and embarrassment. Knowing she instinctively shared in my painful experience cut deep, so I pushed harder, even more motivated to expeditiously shake off such family shame. Adding insult to injury, my son's classmate at his elementary school threw the new story in his face. Ten-year-olds rarely watched news reports, but because some frivolous parent decided to highlight the headline within their household, listening ears turned on. To lessen his angst, I candidly told him, "Son, remember the book I wrote. Your daddy did not do anything wrong, but some people think I did. Regardless, it is not going to impact you." Deep down inside, I emphatically proclaimed to redeem myself. My family deserved that reward.

Being in loved ones' company refueled my drive to escape an uncomfortably imposed proverbial cross. I shifted my mindset, then looked for a way out of this agonizing hellhole. Perhaps a favorable exit strategy from this familiar county would prove advantageous. What pivotal changes were within my reach? How could I take back control of this trajectory? How could I position myself to advance again up the command chain? I put myself on the courthouse stand, mentally pitching resolution proposals or inquiries. During those inquisitive moments, I stepped outside education leadership's realm, approaching the problem as a resourceful man.

Takeaways — Internal Battles Within A Public War

Heavy is the head that wears the crown holds true. Balancing potential risks with ongoing progress and more susceptible losses is no doubt an art. Being a trailblazing leader offers no exemptions from untimely depletion or exhaustion alike. As sporadic obstacles interrupt one's routine, detrimental blows impact one's welfare. Multi-dimensional rejection infused with culminating persecution speaks to traumatic journeys. There are certain lessons only storms or trauma can teach a person, making real-time experience one's best teacher. Unspoken rubrics for dominating a leading life are quite ambiguous. Yet, one's simple success equation is giving each day an individual's best while operating with an integrity-filled, empathetic spirit. Never compromise deeply seated values or dreams for the sake of a title change. Continuously use a strong, sturdy platform to influence needed change for all impacted parties' greater good.

Accidents happen. Adversity transpires. After a reputation's public devaluation or an in-house reprimand, career stocks tank. The damaging effects of this unfavorable circumstance are tenfold. In this sense, a familiar life, whether financially, socially, mentally, or professionally, can literally be flipped upside down within a millisecond. Severe consequences can cost life savings and overall lifestyle. A prospective personal crisis is an inevitable, hard pill to swallow. Since grave side effects are uncontainable, I propose these wise safeguards:

1. Live within means. Fully fund a financial reserve.
2. Honor current job duties and contracted work hours.
3. Always have multiple income streams or certifications.
4. Move with purpose and as a victor, not a victim.
5. Intentionally script the newspaper headline for comeback wins.

Deciding on being a divergent leader is demanding. We are held to higher behavioral standards; it can become taxing. Build a schedule filled with self-care infused with social interactions. Such balanced mixes foment a weapon against self-sabotaging acts or moderate depression. You never get over trauma, but eventually, you learn from it and push forward. Once we move past excruciating pain and shock, we evolve into wiser people. Pay close attention to your current season. Confrontational moments can often be a precursor to exuberant progression. While the First Amendment and a business misstep may have temporarily nailed me to a shameful cross, my faith reminded me that God was not through with me yet. Much like the multi-colored mosaic glass perfectly fits into church house windows, our Creator will put you back together in a more awestriking nature right before people who attempted to shatter dreams or tear you into pieces. Ignore ludicrous opinions others speak against you. God always has the final say. Ready yourself now. Forthcoming future wins will abundantly compensate you for former losses.

"You can have all the degrees in the world, but if you don't have a hustler's mentality, ambition, and common sense, you'll be lost."

Shawn "Jay Z" Carter,
Billionaire Business Owner and
American Rapper

7

The Comeback Motivation

On March 30, 2017, rush-hour traffic morphed into a lengthy deadlock lasting over five hours. One major highway, I-85, among Georgia's busiest highways, unexpectedly crumbled beneath tires rolling along. Miles upon miles of vehicles spanning ninety-two feet disrupted what had been free-flowing routes short moments prior. Drivers were left without connective pavement as dozens nosedived into burning rubble. A pathway engineered to bridge drivers safely and swiftly from point A of Atlanta to point B, plotted across vibrant metro-Atlanta cities in suburbia, disintegrated into two separate roads. It was as if a lightning bolt's flashing fireball had landed; only the fire originated from the darkness below those once-spinning tires. After its multi-million-dollar reconstruction, voluntarily returning to such a frightful place that literally posed life-threatening interruptions now demanded a more profound level of faithfulness and motivation. Simple day-to-day activities like these embody unexpected rollercoaster rides that can leave the greatest leaders flipped upside down, spiraling them back to ground zero. From pursuing historical greatness to breaking generational curses, many setbacks and successes blend transformational leadership journeys. Psychologically, trauma's residual effects associated with demotions or adverse experiences deplete one's emotional well-being, potentially doing long-term damage that may take years to rectify. Akin to running a vehicle on fumes or cheap gas, this distressing fact is incontestable.

Victory and growth, those great pursuits ambitious humans strive to achieve, are dwindled to far-fetched ideas, out of reach, barricaded by powerful adversaries. Upon arriving at this plateau, a leader must either dig deep within, conjuring up revolutionary motivation, or thus find contentment by staying rooted in the same situation. Leaders elect arduous, daunting tasks to rediscover their passionate motivations. Webster's Dictionary defines motivation as the state or condition of being motivated or having a strong reason to act or accomplish something. In fact, those drivers that startling day were probably strongly motivated to reattempt a forty-mile drive to work due to their financial overhead. Such tenacious drive is much more easily embodied when life's struggles are looking up. However, channeling the necessary courage to try again after failure is akin to prying a wounded driver from a five-car pileup with bare hands rather than the jaws-of-life apparatus used by a trained professional.

Even when randomly scanning résumés of one's best opponent and knowing without a shadow of doubt you are ten times more qualified than that professional, it is still hard shaking defeat. Former President Barack Obama's life vividly illustrates such a setback to a successful journey predating his election to our providential country's highest, most esteemed office in our illustrious United States of America: President.

Just a mere one year short of publishing his first memoir, Obama entered the political arena in 1996. Such immersion into a massive limelight placed him, his family, and his decisions under extreme microscopic observation. In lieu of unmerited scrutiny, the populace elected him as representative of District 13 in Illinois' Senate. Hoping he could capitalize on this winning momentum, he placed an election bid for the 1st Congressional District, but he lost. Immediately upon such an unfavorable outcome's initial impact, he was most likely defeated. However, he did not allow this defeat to define him or materialize as his last chance at success within the vast political arena. Yes, he shifted, adjusted, then reentered upcoming races. Undoubtedly, trivial opponents worked at every turn, devaluing his experience and further poking holes through Obama's various reputations. But through it all, he remained steadfast, prudent, and unwavering amidst his forthright, long-sighted mission. Four years later, when 2004 rolled around, he won the US Senate, unseating an incumbent Republican. Then, only four years later, 2008 rolled along on a seemingly smooth track. United States citizens voting Democrat won a majority that defining year, electing him as the first Black president, who would serve eight magnanimous years within our country's White House's many hallowed walls.

While he tugged away at urgent country affairs, a small minority of short-sighted, often biased voters publicly challenged his very citizenship, character, and vision. As almost predicted, being an outlier in a long chain of forty-three former presidents, eight of whom graduated from Harvard like Obama, widened the cracked doors of longtime biased judgment. Breaking news can change headlines, but hardened hearts remain harder to change. That time-tested truth that people never really change holds truer than anything else. Tabloids, white supremacists, and media sources alike worked relentlessly at crucifying Obama almost day by day, dragging his well-endowed résumés through the mud.

He remained visibly in sync with wise wife, attorney, and Yale graduate Michelle Obama's proclamation: "When they go low, we go high." Although a swift, verbal assault is a common reaction to unjust ridicule, he did not employ an eye for an eye, an overused revengeful tactic. He rose above, proving character, grit, and determination to keep going. He had accomplished never-seen-before promotions for Black communities across America. He shined like a true exemplar of maintaining composure, rising above meaningless noise. Naysayers' cacophonous voices fall, reduced to background static. Truth always perseveres, one way or another. The darkest of dark lies have no place when truth crashes through, shining its brightness upon all.

Why is our illustrious former president's story so befitting for this book? Simple. Barack Obama's composed disposition mirrored mine. Regardless of verbal bashing, being called a liar, or suffering a setback, it proved crucial we two Black men remained cool-headed, impactful, and adamant, especially when facing such daunting circumstances. Executing roles typically reserved for our white counterparts meant expectations were easily ten times higher, only growing harder as we climbed our proverbial career ladders. Therefore, we had to run the playbook to the play. There was no margin for error.

Working to rebuild one's reputation and net worth is gruesome, especially when it proves unsafe to allow spectators to see a guy's blood, sweat, and tears. Remember, there are two types of people taking part in your campaign run: those who want to see you win versus those who want to see you remain unchanged or a loser. Such dualities forced me to cleave strongly to my routine. Even if my reacquired ascension took four years like Obama, keeping a consistent flow of mental and physical enrichment was beyond lifesaving oftentimes. I vowed to do what made me feel like the best version of myself, never questioning my decision to take the road less traveled.

Basic training at the sun's first rays echoed my process of pledging. Commitment to crossing as an Omega man snapped back within what felt like minutes. Those college days birthed a more persistent, motivated beast within me as I realized that I alone determined every fruit of my labor, my work's earned outcomes. Fast forward to adulthood, willfully waking up just before 4:00 a.m., hours ahead of America's working majority, provided a still-feasible timeframe to gain a head start during any given day. In the last thirty years, morning swims provided an unrestrained atmosphere for disconnecting from any issues I may have shouldered, releasing dead weight that did not serve me. Once I decompressed, I inhaled deeply, submerging myself in a six-foot pool. Instantly, all noises went silent. Bliss surrounded me. Heavy burdens were lifted as I balanced my weight at the exact intersection where water met air. Life seemed easier during those moments idly treading water. There were no lies teeming at life needing debunking. No errands demanding attention. No applications requiring submission. No students enacting redirecting.

Knowing my story would not end in that current valley's depths, I placed my back against the pool walls, then lifted my hands, palms facing upwards. Intentionally, I set each day's tone, voicing the Serenity Prayer: "God, grant me the serenity to accept the things I cannot change, the courage to change the things that I can, and the wisdom to know the difference. Amen." Those words proved lifesaving wisdom throughout life. I turned to them whenever needed, not ashamed to surrender all to my Creator.

To further regulate blood pressure and any other potential stress-induced ailments, I vigorously hit a few laps around the pool as if Simone Manuel, the first African American woman to win a gold medal in Olympic swimming, was right on my heels. Upon exiting the pool, barely a quarter past five o'clock, I dried off, then suited up. I jumped back into my SUV, dutifully heading toward the county that still paid all those adjusted bills. I was still a leading champion, just stuck between sacrificing the man I was and becoming the man I was designed to be. Remember, divine plans were assigned to your life as you curiously floated inside the protective aquatic environment within your mother's womb. Therapeutic sessions like these at sunrise propelled an energetic climax, fueling me with power and hope. Yes, it remains essential a fellow sometimes identifies seemingly invisible silver linings during desolate times, albeit the discovery replicates the sheer, stark impossibilities of finding a tiny, single needle buried deeply within a teetering haystack.

Surprisingly, life took a positive turn when I made this much-needed mental shift. Internally, I had accepted the worst of the worst. Don't believe it? Take my word. It's true, friend. My name, "Simpson," no longer required prime-time media coverage or graced front pages. No more calamitous consequences would be issued. No added worries for Roxie Simpson's baby boy.

Unless you have children, you can only imagine the pain that a parent endures when they see their child(ren) hurting. The mere utterance of "you'll be alright" was enough. It was almost as if she knew that the grit, perseverance, and resilience existing inside of me would eventually come out. Vengeful, powerful opponents threw their final knockout punch, yet I still had lungs filled with breath to go another round, then another, maybe another. A painful persecution that seemed like punishment extended to a modern-day slave finally terminated. Thank God!

Irrevocably, I reached the demarcation line. I got up off the canvas, dusted off my hands, and took control of destiny, grateful it no longer rested contingent upon misguided, external depositions. Finally, every future endeavor would be heavily predicated on my notable body of hard work and unwavering resilience throughout many years. Energized to fight back and then reclaim my predestined, rightful position, I assumed a posture of great expectation. I readied myself to swing yet again, take greater chances, submit applications, and get back strong in the opportunity's ring.

Again, "work hard and watch good things happen." No doubt, I had to provide a real-life example for my son as I asked that he repeat this quote to me every day. As I explained, baseball is a sport of failure, and out of all sports, it has the highest percentage of failure associated with it. If you didn't know, there is a statistical category for "errors." Humbly, I admit I marvel at my mental stamina. As a few tenured colleagues confessed, many people would have quickly thrown their white towels into that messy mix, surrendering years ago, transitioning into an entirely different industry. A wise teacher at Tucker High randomly pulled yours truly aside one day; I do not know why for sure, but maybe she noticed a different pep in my step. Her spirit of discernment was attuned to the man behind the bow tie and suit, my professional superhero cape.

"Dr. Simpson, your best bet at revenge is your comeback success," she intoned calmly but strongly, gazing directly into my tenacious eyes.

I returned her level gaze, then replied, "Thank you, I absolutely agree." This sentiment was already enveloped within my mind, but her verbal expression sealed the deal even more.

Afterward, I became attuned to other people's behaviors, totally at the opposite end of the spectrum from doubtful minorities. This group focused more on how I handled controversy and rose above everyday chaos instead of what happened to old Simp. I walked amidst painful ridicule through those early days after such a brutal scandal, but I kept my head held high. Soul crushed or not, I never handed those taunts or lies a wooden bat that could potentially permanently break my back. Every day offered a fresh chance to mirror the motivational advice I fervently fed other professionals. Onlookers stood, staring with total admiration because of my poise and resilience.

I refused defeat. I was one's worst nightmare if they wanted that. Simp proved worthy, even during harrowing times.

On Tuesday of the following week, I tuned into spiritual playlists on Sirius XM. I needed deep-seated soul enrichment, which would fertilize this motivation seedling, attempting to break fertile ground. I hoped it would grow into a sturdy opportunity plant, ripe with colorful, tantalizing fruit that could be picked. Then, I could harvest more noteworthy outcomes. To my utter pleasant surprise, award-winning gospel artist, pastor, and graduate of Long Island University, Hezekiah Walker's voice entered those sound waves one gracious day. "They whispered, conspired, they told their lies. God favors me. My character, my integrity, my faith in God, He favors me." At such a pivotal moment as this, I sang along boisterously, holding nothing back like I was a contracted choir member. Our voices blended harmoniously. It seemed providential. Elation consumed every fiber, every nerve, every cell. Blood flowed through veins with renewed vigor, alive again after feeling deader than dead. I clapped with fervor, affirming those sacred truths. More longtime pain and overbearing fear lashings were flushed away, then irrigated, then finally replaced by acknowledgment for God's providential, timely favor upon my very life. What a gift! Modern-day Negro spirituals resonated core-deep within me, giving supernatural strength and fortitude to keep progressing, minute by minute, hour by hour.

Unfortunately, this soulful moment passed, like all moments. As the radio inevitably shifted from one varied melody to the next, I stood firmly in my own truth: Upon striking the right moment, I would move on from this point toward a more rewarding destination. Life is an ever-steady stream, never stopping. It may waver or divert. It could slow. It very well can speed up, but life never stops. Such a fact has burrowed deep within me after all these years. I know there remain many untapped opportunities ahead. A guy simply needs to keep moving. Along life's current? Against it? Perhaps faster than it.

What came next? Well, friend, I spiced things up by adding some diversity to my old routine and reestablished some much-needed earning power. A colleague and friend, Patrick Graham, was one of the most respected and renowned basketball officials in the Southeast. Our relationship began when I offered him a position at Miller Grove High School. I was encouraged to take off one hat, then donned the referee's tried, true cap. I invested precious time and resources to attain a certification untainted by pending red marks on my educator's certificate. After writing a check for $350 that would cover training camp and association fees, I sourced my official uniform, starting with a black whistle. Check. Two collarless, short-sleeved shirts with vertical black and white stripes. Check. Solid black trousers and socks. Check. Recommended, high-performance shoes with black laces manufactured for running. Check. Annual grand total invested for apparel alone: $650. Check, check, check. Eventually, I would work to secure higher-paying high school basketball game jobs, so I meticulously followed the Georgia High School Association wardrobe rules from the onset. Once I was cleared to referee and the equipment arrived, it was time to cash in on my investment every chance I got. That position would flow seamlessly along with daily evening responsibilities while changing my typical environment. Outside of my son's baseball schedule and daddy-daughter dates with my princess, I volunteered to work four or five fall league games under the tutelage of Mr. Graham. During the day, I was a boss. However, on the court, he was mine. He took every opportunity to remind me of that! Any point to be evaluated and illustrate a burgeoning referee career was more than accepted. Being the best at my craft was non-negotiable, putting my name inside the proverbial hat to be hired for the best, most competitive games and most frequent bookings.

However, if I am being frank, this proved a humbling experience. For the first time in a long time, my insecurities skyrocketed as I boldly embarked on a new, rocky territory. At any given moment, visiting teams could morph into angry lobbyists if I made an honest call favoring our home school. Of course, naysayers would fail, seeing it as forthright. Contrarily, if I made calls that pushed our home team closer to true victory, half the gym's occupants would yell supporting words from bleachers, even from the nosebleeds. Being a novice referee literally reflected election night angst — during those last, pivotal hours, I could become their preferred candidate for the following game or a never-again-selected officiant. Thankfully, one particular seasoned referee told me that if you keep up your pace, blow your whistle with utmost confidence, plus become one with every basketball game, your job will flow far more naturally than if you freeze up, lack confidence, or distance yourself from the game. In the voice of Patrick Graham, "Listen, Simp, pretend you have on a black and white striped bowtie. Teleport yourself to those school hallways you seamlessly manage. The basketball court is no different from the high schools you run." The parallelisms were evident when I stepped back to assess. For example, deescalating teenagers fighting over a cute girl was like mediating verbal battles between two infuriated coaches. Every game, I would close my eyes, then envision what he told me. It helped me navigate this new territory, especially getting me through even more dreadful games.

But in complete transparency, game time proved no place where I could be anything less than stellar on the court. After all, this seasoned referee assured me that no one other than me would notice I was a rookie, so any crowd would respect my calls. More than ten years later, that timely career I branched out to explore still serves me quite well. It is a decision I do not regret making even once. Such choices more than show you never know how a certain decision may affect life in tremendously beneficial ways.

As fate would have it, just when my barren cup showed positive signs of being refilled, a trusted mentor fell into a deep pit hole full of harsh, unrelenting public scrutiny. No one is above reproach, it seems. I could hardly conceive what these tired ears heard when I first found out such information. Various news sources stated this bishop had haphazardly built an unprofessional relationship with a church member. When this rumor started, I had known this ordained minister, father, and philanthropist for over ten years. Consequently, I held my friend in high esteem. I had never questioned his character or judgment, not once. What reason would I have? None. However, our history did not matter. This play of unfair crucifixion proved all too familiar. I knew it like my hand. History repeated like an old record on replay, doomed to spin forever. There it was again, the law's court, then public opinion of the court.

Perhaps surrounding myself with illustrious, sincere, stalwart men who decided to be exceptions to perpetuating statistics will inevitably come under attack at some point. Only time will tell. Nonetheless, I rose from ashes, born anew, ready, willing, even joining his church while hundreds upon hundreds of members flocked away faster than legendary superhero Black Lightning from well-known DC Comics. I can attest that our culture can be quite unforgiving, far too quick to quit on an unsuspecting guy like me. Allegations, whether true or false, can destroy a person who is otherwise untarnished utterly and completely.

Abandonment is like throwing salt into a gaping open wound, leaving it festering with unfounded pain, only deepening hurt. Once Bishop noticed my prompt display of immense, unwavering support, he remembered why he chose me as a chair for NB Christian Academy. Little did he know, empowering him at one of his lowest points, such a notorious public humiliation episode also empowered yours truly.

Each time we extend empathy and grace to people at hard, unforgiving rock bottom, we become strengthened to surmount our own personal mountains. Then we are bolstered, climbing higher still than ever before. Throughout our unpredictable lives, we will go through many valleys, but these nail-biting pits rife with unfamiliar territory are just a teachable pit stop. Every opportunity can prove a learning moment if allowed. We must, by our grit, sweat, blood, and tears, by any means necessary, pull from any proverbial cross of daggering pain. Fully engaging our intrinsic motivation, we take one step forward, then another. Yes, we must persevere until we attain our next targeted goal planted deep, true, and strong at our mountaintop: our deserved, desired destination. Do not give up, friend. Keep going against all odds. Even when everything feels impossible, only a tiny spark is needed. Then even a man lower than he has gone before can reignite hope within, shining light so all may see.

Takeaways - Yield To Innate Motivation

South Africa's former president, Nelson Mandela, once proclaimed, "It always seems impossible until it's done." Imagine if one never believed we could build a submarine or if the Wright brothers never pursued their idea of flying airplanes. Experiencing our world as we know it would be mundanely confined to horses and carriages, cars, buses, and trains, plus continental borders holding us back. Life as we know it depended upon these illustrious leaders consistently shattering what once seemed like glass ceilings. Fortunately, divergent thinkers like these greats mentioned above made a society-shifting decision to remain motivated, failure after failure, until pre-set objectives were realized into reality.

Upon arrival at the cross-section between past trials and future triumphs, a leader reaches a fork in the road. Here, there are two motivation lanes, navigating a person toward starkly different lives. One lane is pursued by a leader dependent upon extrinsic motivation, such as money, titles, and recognition. Any motives rooted in this dependency cause this leader to transform into a zombie-walking automaton, lacking a purpose-filled life. No gumption to progress any further along life's long path is present. No reason for getting out of their beds each morning is stirred. If they are not careful, a motivation drought's extended time period can send these people spiraling into a deeply depressive state, where they forego years of their lives because they were stuck living in the past. They were not glued to their promise. A U-turn is desperately needed A.S.A.P. Golden, intrinsic motivation securely paves our other lane. Such motivation is a true asset for living a life filled with purpose. Not only does this internal drive serve as a moral compass, but it also mitigates dangerous codependency on outside forces and evaluations. The beauty of self-motivation is that it seamlessly marries hard work and hope. It is like a vow, an everlasting promise made. Armed with these truths, a person can step into their future empowered, ready, and victorious.

To cultivate a winning legacy that will ultimately catalyze our country at its very core, assume an authentic leadership role, come heaven, hell, or apartheid-level high waters. As you acknowledge your rightful emotions, then sit with feelings, amplify that powerful voice and forthright purpose. Even as you ponder upon mile markers casting light on decisions that torched your trajectory, do not waste resources aimed at undoing your past. Each situation made you a better, stronger version of yourself. Forgive yourself for inevitable detours. If you stay the course long enough, then you open a better, more opportune door to receive "double for your trouble." How is that for compensatory damages? Such a well-earned, magnanimous blessing only serves its role as a redemptive power when you decide to rewrite the way your burgeoning story goes, taking the lean to pen its next best chapter. Your intrinsic value is ten times greater than any misstep or mere error witnessed by external parties. Only you can assign permanent denotation to be associated with your name. Allow such motivation to continue to resurface.

Motives for pursuing audacious goals become crystal clear given enough time, patience, and effort. Reestablish a routine that allows you to fortify your mental, spiritual, and physical states. Redemption is a tangible byproduct of motivation and persistence. Ready yourself for ever-emerging, unseen, unexpected plot twists. Challenge physical limits visible to our naked eyes, then explore hidden possibilities lurking around every corner. You have the final say. Start clapping for yourself now because your comeback will undoubtedly be more than monumental. It will be at that mountaintop peak, climbed one step at a time. Rest assured. Victory awaits.

"Making your mark on the world is hard. If it were easy, everybody would do it. But it's not. It takes patience. It takes commitment and it comes with plenty of failure along the way."

Barack H. Obama
44th President of the United States,
Movie Producer and Philanthropist

FROM DEMOTION TO PROMOTION

DR. RALPH L. SIMPSON

8

Spark of Redemption

Between 1950 and 1969, financial disparities combined with illegal drug influxes, brutally and unforgivingly dismantled family structures across the United States. Undoubtedly, the most vulnerable groups feeling the blunt forces of these antagonistic, ruthless sledgehammers were low-income Black children. They were everywhere, inner city or small town; few escaped such seemingly harsh punishment for a crime they did not commit. On a large scale, society wrote off these groups, seeing their recovery process as an impossible feat. Yet, in 1968, one child psychiatrist, Dr. James Comer, challenged such a discriminatory narrative. He launched a restorative program in New Haven, Connecticut's slums. These African American citizens attended underperforming schools, falling into extremely low-income brackets. However, this visionary worked to give these forgotten students a spark of hope. Partnering with the esteemed Yale Child Study Center, Dr. Comer highlighted positive achievement, attendance, and behavior of student bodies within these learning establishments were inclined to exhibit under exemplary leadership.

Such a holistic approach certainly mirrored my mantra, "Reach before you teach." Before a child can master a standard, any competent leader must go beyond surface-level academic expectations and understand who the child is. Hence, without a doubt, social-emotional wellness begets academic excellence in that exact order. Take a gander at statistics. An irrefutable correlation between social-emotional learning and student outcomes is quite prevalent, which becomes visibly evident in school settings. Improved academic performance and mental wellness produce a better school climate, inclusive of polished social skills. Educating a healed, content, contributing member of society starts before a teenager's first job or graduation. Students can only successfully transition to adulthood with these intrinsic competencies intact and ingrained deep within their youthful minds. However, a question inevitably arises. But what happens when elected officials disregard schools desperate for social-emotional enrichment and work culture overhaul?

Schools become a dead man's zone, a juvenile's graveyard filled with deferred dreams, a breeding ground rife with generational curses. Such mortifying outcomes are historically visible when metropolitan schools outperform more rural ones. Contrarily, Rover High was an outlier. According to *US News*, this school ranked #13,000 to 17,000 nationally, #216 state-wide. These statistics are catastrophic since our southern state only has a mere 524 public high schools. When it boiled down to student achievement and outcomes, Rover High School hung on by a solitary, thin thread, ready to snap, over an invisible swamp looming with proverbial alligators. One wrong turn and money-hungry investors stood ready to demolish its building, then flip it into multi-family housing. Via the lens of gentrification, underperforming schools are deemed primetime real estate for hungry, greedy developers. Out of twenty-seven public high schools within DeKalb County, Rover was at the deep barrel's bottom, nearing a complete shutdown at any given moment. Fear rested right around the corner, ready to pounce.

Upon reaching my second year as an AP at Troy High School, my leadership acumen circulated the county again. A positive wildfire resulted that time around, making a beautiful redemption from formerly desecrated ashes. Can you imagine the phoenix rising? That is what I hope you see. Additionally, any colleague privy to my skillsets questioned decision-makers, "Are you going to take him out of timeout?" Being placed on timeout was the season attached to a professional who experienced leave with pay or a rare demotion. Resilience seated deep inside me reassured those still in education that I could only be a better leader after not drowning in misery. By them rallying around me at that lowest professional leadership position, I sensed a turnaround waited right around any corner. No longer could county leaders brush aside outcries. Yet, I kept rebuilding life as I knew it, day by day, gig by gig.

Two years had elapsed since I conducted any business activity, but inflation and innate ambition made that dormant state short-lived. While I drove home one Friday evening, I received a call from a well-known pastor in Clayton County. Reverend Keith Reynolds was a retired DeKalb County principal. He extended an offer to deliver a twenty-minute motivational speech to his congregation. The vision was to seamlessly marry leadership components for a revolutionary life — skills, integrity, and agape love. Of course, I accepted the offer without hesitation, deeming it a visible reminder of untapped potential.

On that contracted Sunday, I shared my story with an eager audience, then asked them to identify key pillars of having "The SIMPle Factor," distinguishing traits that clearly set one apart from the rest. In closing, I encouraged each attendee to see beyond current circumstances and never fall victim to a common fallacy that God has abandoned a person just because they find themselves in a dark tunnel or valley. This business engagement was a grand slam. I hit that ball out of the park! My gratification mirrored sentiments I had when I opened a brand-new, state-of-the-art high school for the county in 2010 named Mercy High.

During the previous five years, Hurricane Katrina's traumatizing damage caused an influx of students to relocate to

Clayton and Dekalb. Both counties direly needed new schools to mitigate overcrowded classrooms plus any brewing lawsuits. Hence, DeKalb decision-makers opened their administration pool to assess their current human capital. At that time, ten teachers within each school building conducted peer evaluations. These randomly selected professionals rated their administrators' ability at leadership and yielding results. Principals like me entered our names into the pool, then also completed oral interviews. After tallying composite scores, I was the frontliner who was chosen to spearhead a new school opening.

Centered between two rivalling high schools, Mercy High School would open its doors to freshmen and sophomores, yours truly serving as its very first principal. Being trusted with such a merger was an opportunity I treated with immense diligence and care. I sourced and hired over 90% of the staff, building a natural work climate that would promote loyalty and hard work. With buy-in, we hammered down and crafted our school identity.

I grew up just a rock throw away from The Atlanta University Center—home to Spelman, Interdenominational Theological Center, Morehouse, Clark Atlanta, and Morehouse School of Medicine. Luckily, my formative years took place against the backdrop of Black excellence and collegiate success. Although each school was exceptional, attracting students worldwide, I grew a deep affinity for the Morris Brown College Marching Wolverine Band. Hence, I pitched these same school colors, purple and silver, to my team. What would be their initial thoughts? Would they get on board with my vision?

By a landslide decision, we collectively modelled our newly founded high school as a replica of Morris Brown. Now, hopeful scholars who formerly bled blue and gold pride from their home schools would receive a blood transfusion, if you will. Each enrolled student would now proudly bleed purple and silver. Former Bulldogs and Raiders would breed to become powerful, fighting Wolverines. I was on cloud nine, but the college itself was at ground zero. What was the stimulus of this disparity? It had recently lost its accreditation due to debt and other financial challenges, placing it within a magnanimous bind along with other historically black college and university closures. You might assume I allowed such a fact to dim my spirit. However, no temporary demotion or reputation blemish would stifle my overall love for it. Imagine our staff's moment of hope when I commissioned them to assist our band director in the creation of our school hymn.

From the onset, our newly built team completed a S.W.O.T. analysis of the school because it was a business. A strength was we were building our school with research-proven strategies strongly linked to success. Additionally, we only accepted first- or second-year students, giving our newly crafted student body a fair chance at bonding. By the same token, launching a new school goes head-to-head with kickstarting a business. Weaknesses and challenges were plentiful. Students entered ninth-grade year lacking many friends, but many strangers, former rivals, surrounded them. Most parents worked one or two jobs to adequately cope with the recent economic recession. This fact, however, presented another golden opportunity to teach children how to maximize their potential by treating school as a full-time job.

On the flip side, a major threat to our success was receiving higher-ups' disapproval for implementing new tactics with hopes of getting a better result. Secondly, failure at establishing an "it takes a village" commitment would no doubt equate to substandard outcomes. So, as a unified brigade, we attacked the latter head on my second year. Our Annual Yearly Progress (AYP) scores, metrics that decided school funding or closures based on certain metrics, were not excellent that first year. Were this guy's envisioned golden standards too high? Perhaps, but shooting for the stars out the gate was an optimal tactic to quickly establish momentum. Hence, we proactively switched gears, taking massive action and organizing a school-based protest for parental engagement.

During four consecutive days, staff and I took to the streets, adding four extra hours to our regular workday. Before school commenced and after student dismissal, Monday through Thursday, we rang the proverbial alarm for parents, saying effectively, immediately, "Wake up! Jump into your child's academic world." At sunrise each day, female teachers ran our protest. Then, male teachers took the evening shift while the sun lowered, signaling another day's end. Chivalrous acts were always interwoven in my leadership style — just like the Southern gentleman I am. From start to finish, everything ran like a well-oiled machine. To top it all off, Wednesday night, we had a lock-in and hit city streets until midnight struck. Talk about commitment; let this be an anecdote to shine a light on the truth that educators do not get enough credit or pay. But I digress, hoping my passion for elevating future leaders' and family success rubs off on you a little, too.

Much to our pleasant surprise, that Thursday's parent-teacher conference made local history. Hundreds of parents magnanimously stepped up to the plate, ready at bat, if you will, joining us. Together, united, we pursued giving today's pupils the best shot at lifetime success. Parents were schooled on their child's academic DNA, from their test scores to course grades. Then, we transitioned to the gym. I advised parents and students on how important it is to attend school, plus academic performance. Yes, surely, I shared just a snippet of my story's journey from remediation courses to a remarkable career. By night's end, I was 100% certain that there was no way these students' academic wellness would not improve after this historical, rallying day. Such a bold move at establishing a strong family engagement foundation could have very well backfired, but our gutsy move definitely paid a handsome return on investment that would pay dividends long down the road. Stronger community connection was achieved. Better student performance was achieved. The protest goal was achieved. This four-day campaign transformed our entire school's culture for the better. Check, check, check. What's next?

When I juxtaposed that remarkable success with my second ascension, I understood it would take the most challenging assignments to get the most rewarding comebacks. I would need to resuscitate a formerly euthanized, forgotten school. I started beneath the surface, tilling the proverbial land to make it fertile ground again, ready to plant seeds, then water, and watch hopeful scholars grow into tomorrow's leaders. Proving myself all over again would be a game repulsive to any rookie leader. I never backed down from a shot at redemption. The county was relentlessly throwing me to hungry wolves headfirst.

Year after year, stifling challenges within Rover High School's walls knocked out brave leaders within record time. Administrators who accepted a leadership role here were either entering retirement, surviving a demotion, or redeeming themselves after termination. Sadly, people rarely arrived or left on good terms. It was as if this school was the very place where administrators came to hang their careers and die. I could not, would not accept that fate. I would be their eighth principal in eight years to attempt changes this underperforming student body so desperately needed. I, Dr. Simpson, stood ready to champion a magnanimous turnaround. It was now grind mode. Time to amplify my deeply seated beliefs about restorative practices and student achievement. If turning a school around was a sport, I would be recognized as a resounding MVP.

First impressions are proven, timeless, great indicators that demonstrate workplace culture and student performance alike. Rover High had been notoriously known as a school bearing disenfranchised, neglected fruit, given compounded years of combined poverty and neglect. These truths were evident when I approached such an old, nearly dilapidated education building. The marquee, an electronic device that serves as a billboard for the schools' vision, appeared antiquated. Making matters worse, its flashing message that read, "Report cards will be sent home on May 31st" had a few words misspelled. If this welcoming message wrapped in grammatical errors set the tone, then I could only imagine what academic achievement levels or bars were being set inside that sad-looking infrastructure. I shook my head, utter disappointment coursing through me, vowing I would make that message correction a top objective for day one.

After I assessed Rover High's front presentation, I drove around its building, identifying any potential modifications desperately needed to enrich any educational experience. My jaw dropped. Not only were its athletic fields neglected and poorly manicured, but baseball fields looked condemned. How could anyone practice the carefully honed art of hitting a homerun if the very grounds appeared like Michael Jackson's music video, *Thriller*? I inhaled deeply, accepting the harrowing fact that I would be the leader who would slay proverbial dragons of despair on day one.

After parking in the assigned principal space, I looked at my rearview mirror, then paused. A step toward redemption was upon me. Finally, profuse bleeding from post-traumatic stress slowly lessened deep inside. I ascended one rung at a time, my worst days behind me. Despite Rover High's long-running history filled with negative outcomes, I would treat such an opportunity as a chance for everyone to start from a fresh slate. Not only did I accept this challenge, but I also realized my successful track record. It came from years when I worked hard, giving everything I had. If I could build Mercy High from ground zero with immense success, then I could breathe life into Rover High.

Feeling a deep-seated pride, I rolled up invisible proverbial sleeves. I ensured my purple bowtie was perfectly placed, then beeped my key fob, setting the car's alarm. Then, I marched into the front office, sporting my chocolate Derbies plus heaps of faith. Unfortunately, a putrid stench soaked in the festering front office's walls immediately rudely interrupted my short-lived, pleasant outlook. Whether it stemmed from mold or simply lackadaisical standards' awful reek, this was beyond unacceptable.

The secretary greeted me with a warm welcome, lilting her voice, but a chilling sense of disappointment muted her voice when I caught sight of a 5x5 carpet stain preceding my office door. You got to be kidding me. How could she work efficiently during modern times using a computer system hailing from the early nineties?

While I toured the building's interior, I noticed some classrooms bore aging roof leaks and flood-line marks. Had any county funding been allocated to this school's needs, or had it all been written off entirely? I remained cordial, but internal discontent burned hot. Topping it off, twenty-five teacher openings remained unfilled. No wonder a negative perception attached itself to Rover High. Why would any student take pride in being a Rover Raider when neglect raided what could be a promising learning establishment under different conditions?

In no time flat, I had a crystal-clear understanding of what needed to be done. Let's flip this tainted trajectory, turning it into a much more promising one. Logistically, the whole structure needed more modern technology. On our human capital side, several open positions needed filling. Clearly, educators had run for the hills after having a near-death experience with that education system.

On the first day of school, I stopped by QuikTrip to grab a quick coffee. A police officer asked, "Where are you now?"

I smiled with pride. "I'm at Rover."

His jaw hung open. He shook his head. "Good luck with that!"

I already knew what thoughts conjured up his well wishes. But I would no doubt transform Rover's tainted reputation. "How much time you got?" He followed me to the school and was downright floored.

Before the students arrived, he and I strolled into Rover High as if the Lakeside Band were doing a live exhibition of *Fantastic Voyage*. Walking into Rover High proved a renewed journey against the backdrop of repaired roof leaks, freshly painted bathrooms, a fully staffed school, and updated technology. Our V103 media family, Hank Stewart Foundation, churches, plus other community partners helped my team curate a red-carpet welcome-back affair. The band played upbeat tunes while we rolled out red construction paper at the entry. New Birth sent two hundred members to make this first-day epic. The telling hour arrived to put our would-be esteemed school back on the map better than ever. I addressed the student body by reviewing the two most violated school rules. We would follow these, no questions asked. No exceptions.

1. No rude or disrespectful behavior.
2. Follow instructions without fail.

Our first PTSA meeting was a disaster. Only four of one thousand parents attended. However, one simple ploy would send students running home to grab these missing parents — uniforms. During the last block, I made an announcement.

"Starting Monday, all students will be required to wear uniforms."

Yes, it is another gutsy move that would totally disrupt business as usual. Although I delivered the order as a tactic to increase parental involvement, the risk proved another win. Some students confessed excitement at wearing uniforms. At our next parent meeting, we had double-digit attendance. Forty parents arrived. They cosigned my announcement, sharing an alarming call for a positive school identity. Hence, we transformed this risk into a collective effort. Students and staff organized a fashion show that would display different wardrobe options. For the upcoming semester, we would focus on unified bottoms: black or khaki. Undoubtedly, the students' welfare monopolized my winter break. I could barely sleep, knowing some students did not have the resources to buy uniforms. Hence, I reached out to my trusty network again. Generous people donated skirts, pants, and shirts of all sizes. Contrary to what a former administrator cautioned me, "remember where you work," I pulled off another facelift no one deemed would be possible.

The second semester began. I stood ready to receive these refreshed pupils after an initial holiday reset. With anticipation, I imagined at least fifty percent would proudly sport new uniforms. Two buses arrived. Shockingly, every student wore a uniform. They looked unified, professional, and proud. I gave myself a proverbial standing ovation for evoking that change. I also managed my expectation for our entire student body to follow suit. Much to my delighted surprise, students piled off the preceding buses dressed for success, restoring depleted school pride. Inevitably, fifteen or twenty students challenged the change. No surprise there. A few will always disobey. But with one phone call to their parents, they were marching purchased uniforms to the building's entrance within an hour. Every student eventually complied. By the upcoming fall, we integrated tops, giving our hopeful scholars options. They could personalize their looks if they wanted. No other public school had attempted or succeeded at such a unifying measure. Consequently, the Rover brand, as we knew it, would take on a more positive, elite status.

As my first year concluded, I reflected on notable glows and outstanding growth. Naturally, I sought out ways of improving student experiences and staff satisfaction even more. I strived to be fully prepared for next year. The same twenty-five teachers I sourced from recruiting affairs hosted within our school cafeteria signed on again: another promised year. The same pupils who society counted out due to unaddressed social and emotional traumas experienced double-digit growth in graduation rates. Behind the scenes, I pushed myself to make this run as principal the best one yet, even if that meant leading a school deemed to be at the very bottom. Between surveys and accolades, the region nominated me as principal of the year. Then, to add even more icing on my redemption cake, our entire surrounding county, yes, you guessed right — the very same one responsible for my demotion, voted me as the district's principal of the year. Talk about irony! Wearing this crown felt heavier this time around while I experienced my second shot at success under even more watchful eyes. Sure, witnessing people rally behind me again evoked immeasurable gratification. Yet this second ascension proved also more personal, a fresh opportunity. I would walk in my God-given purpose, a better man, a better leader. Surely, Mom beamed proudly, thanking God for her baby boy's redemption.

After being honored at those fall ceremonies, I reengaged with my home school, developing a new action plan to yield even better results than the previous year. I grabbed a blue pen from my top desk drawer and then started analyzing data. Another S.W.O.T. analysis would give me insights into what worked well or what needed some fine-tuning. Looking at the strengths uncovered by shaping a village-like scholarly culture, I applauded myself. The MVP of leadership had hit a few homeruns. I had struck a few curveballs out of the park, even. Before I could address weaknesses, I received a phone call from another district office. The Interim Superintendent, Michael Thurmond, offered me a new position, Regional Superintendent. My head dropped in awe of such divine order. I maintained my cool, accepting the amazing offer. I proudly handed the baton to a current AP who I had molded.

Shockingly, I relocated to the SAME address and SAME office with the SAME responsibilities. The only two differences were a slight pay increase, given inflation, and a new, more challenging region I would manage. Now, I would walk it as I talk it — being an exemplar of hard work and motivation.

Takeaways - Leverage Your Redemptive Momentum

As fellow Atlanta native, the esteemed Dr. Martin Luther King Jr. once proclaimed, "Change does not roll in on wheels of inevitability but comes through continuous struggle." When life becomes smooth sailing too fast, leadership aptitudes simultaneously take a nosedive. A little struggle or controversy evokes an innate power to be better. When it seems like all forces are working against you or you cannot regain your footing, take a pause. Go back to your home plate and reflect on your current circumstances. Count the progressive steps. Identify any chastening hurdles. Then, grab a pen and complete a S.W.O.T. analysis of the vision you are pursuing. Get crystal clear on the strengths you can leverage and a few weaknesses you will work to polish. After this needed, introspective session, ready yourself for the best opportunities. Assume the armor of God as you prepare for an ascension to greater heights.

Opportunities are a dime a dozen, but only a select few are worthy of your gifts or time. In the process of rebuilding, fortify your emotional intelligence as you enter unfamiliar territory. Contrary to the popular mantra that the third time is a charm, getting another shot at glory can also cause harm. Such damage can be inflicted on an unsuspecting person's psyche while they slowly walk on invisible eggshells, careful not to crack a recovering reputation. Conversely, a leader who opts to make their second or third chance the best journey wins on a large scale. Just take a gander at the firing and rehiring of Apple's CEO, Steve Jobs. No matter the demotion, your reputation makes you invaluable human capital. As momentum from small wins and overall buy-in escalates, so does the internal motivation to make powerful strides. Redemption is a blessing, not an expectation. Everyone is not afforded this graceful opportunity, even if they are more than deserving. So, maximize your redemptive momentum and make great things happen.

"Damn right I like the life I live, 'cause I went from negative to positive."

Christopher "The Notorious B.I.G." Wallace, American Rapper and Ghostwriter

FROM DEMOTION TO PROMOTION

DR. RALPH L. SIMPSON

Final Words

Glorious Reconciliation

Life's journey illustrates the resounding power of second chances. Peruse a Hall of Famers list of legendary leaders like Sha'Carri Richardson, Rocky Balboa, Michael Jordan, Michael Vick, and Barack Obama. Quickly, you will glean that many historical figures did not defer their dreams after a single hurdle. Whether they were being ejected from the home team or shunned by fans, these tenacious individuals evolved as people and sharpened their skills. Then, in perfect timing, they showed up and got it right the second time. For me, everything finally came full circle in 2014. Although a pool of tears infiltrated every fiber of my being, I could not cry. Overwhelming joy plugged those tears as my life story's most gruesome chapter approached a culminating period. Yes, a period, like a sentence's end. During too many previous years, another unexpected semicolon continued to prolong that season. Some powers-to-be kept penning my trajectory, but now I was completely restored. As the sole pen holder, I would correctly dictate my narrative over the next two years.

Undeniably a wiser visionary, I took up better leadership roles placed against a far worse backdrop. My newly acquired region led the county in suspension rates. Historically, I was known for running a tight ship. Standards of excellence would remain prevalent. As an added layer, I worked toward being a walking torch carrier who rallied for second chances, also known as restorative practices. Leveraging a much-needed added certification in this area, I constantly encouraged leaders to employ a village-minded approach. This holistic tactic was ten times more advantageous to focus on the doer or child and its impact on the class leader or teacher. Collectively, we orchestrated a process that would mend classroom relationships while simultaneously holding every student accountable. Between coaches, parents, administrators, teachers, and sponsors, each child's second chance could be backed by an action-based resolve. People are far from perfect and are obviously bound to make mistakes. To err is human, after all. It was my esteemed, rightful duty as a regional leader to wrap these errors in forgiveness and learning experiences alike.

Statistically, males were suspended four times as much as females. I returned to my old trusty strategy room, looking up to great leaders who could tackle this problem head on. No way would I sit back, watching the school-to-prison pipeline live within those family lineages. No, not anymore. This sad, sad, cyclical narrative needed to stop. In 2014, then-President Barack Obama launched an initiative, "My Brother's Keeper Task Force." Like me, he refused to turn a blind eye to inequitable structures weighing heavily on Black and Brown males. I championed this program, spearheading it in DeKalb County. This community, amongst 250 others across our great nation, committed to creating a cradle-to-college or career pathway for marginalized groups. Over forty school districts reformed discipline procedures, a small drop in the bucket, sure, but as more schools adopt this needed program, it will surely make positive waves of change that are long overdue. In my county alone, I noticed a huge, paradigm shift in our educational practices and student outcomes. These results promise a better future, but more must be done.

Within twenty-four months, school climates went from winter gloom to summer lights. Suspension rates in twenty-three schools I managed dropped by 25%. Test scores and attendance averages increased. Comparatively, graduation rates showed a positive correlation. These results speak for themselves. Once again, my reputation was primetime news across the education circuit. However, this time, the truth and results marked it well. No one could deny the validity of transformational leadership when it stared them straight in the face.

After watching my daughter cheer during one particular Friday night football game, Dr. Beasley, a former senior administrator in DeKalb, called. The two of us had cemented a strong, professional relationship since 2000, when we both stepped into educational leadership roles. At the time, he boldly led Clayton County, crafting a prominent key role on his team. It was yet to be filled. Before he could share the salary and any attached benefits, I verified his knowledge of my stained educator's certificate. He glossed over it, fully aware that governing systems desperately needed some fine-tuning. After receiving board approval, Beasley quarterbacked me to a top-tier position. Once again, it was this gentleman's duty to create a promising narrative, not just for one school, but sixty-five. My toolbox and track record alone eased any anxiety as I found solace in running through any plays Beasley or I devised. What an opportunity! I would not let these educational institutions down. Many promising scholars' futures depended on it.

Clayton County was rich with elite educators, compassionate leaders, and ambitious children. Yet, this district fell victim to negative headlines that worked to depreciate marginalized areas. According to SchoolDigger rankings, Clayton County fell in Georgia's bottom quartile of 201 school districts. I did not fret; Omega men like me just stepped up to the plate. All too familiar with misleading statistics and erroneous projections, I proudly accepted the position as Deputy Superintendent of School

Leadership and Improvement. Resuscitating erroneously labeled underdogs had morphed into a professional sport, and I batted high averages. More importantly, I secured another opportunity to fulfill life's purpose, minimizing educational and economic disparities amongst 50,000 plus students. During that time, this county had inherited numerous Hurricane Katrina survivors dating back to 2005 and had their accreditation hanging in the balance. In 2008, this unfortunate area became notoriously known as the first district nationwide to lose its accreditation in 40 years. Georgia's accreditation entity microscopically scrutinized all public schools, threatening to revoke other districts' accreditations, including Warren County. What if decision-makers took a quick pause to lift the hood and understand the fullness of each school district before inducing traumatic consequences? Just as I had regained my old job, it was equally invigorating to be part of a county that had regained its full accreditation. Talk about inspiration! A chance to help them capitalize on a second chance while healing from trauma was invigorating.

After keenly assessing the county's perils and citizens' plights landscapes, I employed the exact same outcome-producing programming that had led to previous successes. The first base objective would be curating a positive school culture and climate. Each administrator had the power to create the storyline they wanted for how outsiders would read their school. To make landmark changes occur, rituals and routines had to be done like clockwork, no exceptions. This principle stood at the core of high-performing educational institutions. At second base rested relationship management. I even employed the county to create fourteen Student Engagement Specialist positions. It was crucial I met these families where they were. Then, we could roll out social-emotional initiatives. It remained impossible to inject standard-based learning into a child's psyche without tending to their whole selves first. Some scholars had experienced life-threatening events and were now knee-deep in a global pandemic. Talk about never-ceasing quicksand. To combat these truths, we channeled their resilience and intelligence, then mapped out a holistic learning process. Thirdly, we met students where they were – online. We were flexible, inventive, and genuine in our approach.

Occasionally, when the work week concluded, frustrating flashbacks monopolized my thoughts. Unfortunately, even amid exceptional triumph, trauma is never 100% eradicated. No survivor is ever the same. Actually, the side effects of rejection and crucifixions resurface each year I replead my case to governing professional commissions. Should I even be surprised anymore? Ironically, at a leadership summit, I initiated an unplanned dialogue with a former director of the Georgia Professional Standards Commission. Although he had retired, he was certainly familiar with my story, especially given my annual call for an expungement of my records. To date, this sanction remains on my certificate. However, given my "good behavior" for over thirteen years post-investigation, previous remarks and injustices should no longer negatively impact my professional livelihood. Was this just another rigged system interwoven in the land of the free and brave? It seemed so. I mean, presidents and popes alike can commit actual crimes, yet they stay in their leadership positions with no future constraints on their successes. Though this is a frustrating fact, I will continue that battle, but I will focus my best efforts on family time and changing lives instead. Why keep fighting a losing battle when I have already won? I know what is true. I know myself. I can stand proudly on dignity and self-respect, knowing embittered folks with lackluster goals will always exist. I encourage you to ignore their fruitless ploys. Rather than seeking a degree of pre-trauma sameness, find contentment in being an elevated version of who you are deep inside.

Upper leadership begets leisure activities where you can revel in your comeback. Walking the green with corporate executives during 70-degree weather, I discovered golf could serve as a staple sport for anyone scaling success ladders or bouncing back from a career blow. Headlines and outsiders only see men at the pinnacle, but conversations exchanged beside each hole unveil defeated leaders who once stood behind a blemished reputation. Choosing to be above average is a daily uphill battle when some days you get a hole-in-one like pro-golfer Tiger Woods. Yet, on days when the wind and world blow in contrasting directions to the direction you are pursuing, your handicap is notoriously low, placing your outcomes on the opposite end of number one.

The SIMPle Factor is your "it" factor – a conglomerate of innate strength and unique gifts that lead to satisfactory results across life's gamut of arenas. In transitioning from your trauma to triumph, employ these steps:

1. Go back to the basics and keep things simple.
2. Uncap a substantial, steady supply of perseverance.
3. Decide to be an ordinary person equipped to do extraordinary things.
4. Be your brother or sister's keeper, supporting a key group of like-minded people.
5. Know that every atomic being has a dormant season and a fruitful one.
6. Expect your comeback to be sweet, exceeding your grandest expectations.

Remember, each day presents a remarkable opportunity for broadening your horizons and multiplying your net worth. Take each day with a fresh perspective, a deep breath, and hope. Never allow anyone to rob you of your innate gifts. You alone remain in control of your destiny. Your outlook is everything. What you envision inside becomes your reality outside. You got this, friend.

Daily, I instinctively embody The SIMPle Factor. Whether taking a MARTA train ride to a Falcon's game or guest speaking at a local organization, I am always in good company with good people. By measuring passersby's smiling faces or grateful embrace when we cross paths, I know my positive footprint is present in ten thousand lives. In fact, the very same county that demoted me turned around and named a street in my honor, Dr. R. L. Simpson Drive. Furthermore, an organic measure of my character is by the fruits of my biological seeds, Chandler and Skyla. Between hitting homeruns or nailing the best cheerleader's toe touches, these two scholars make things happen without skipping a beat. These two stand their ground as natural-born leaders. As reflected by their tenacious hearts and authentic characters, I've done fatherhood quite well. If nothing else, I can stand proud upon this accomplishment. It should be the bedrock upon which I build my legacy. On days when I doubt my self-worth based on traumatic seasons, I can turn to this solid truth: My children are tomorrow's voices, tomorrow's victors. Those two, in tangent with every child born into this perplexed world, are the reason I fight.

It is an undeniable truth that I have left an indelible mark on countless people. This realization alone is a lifetime achievement that supersedes any promotion. There are things accolades cannot buy, such as truth, which cannot be bought with lies or deception. I will always know who I am. I have battle scars to prove it. That chapter has been rewritten, and my story continues.

Let the redacted headline read, "He came. He worked. He got in good trouble."

The end.

FROM DEMOTION TO PROMOTION

DR. RALPH L. SIMPSON

For booking services and book purchases, contact

The SIMPle Factor, LLC.

FROM DEMOTION TO PROMOTION

NOTES